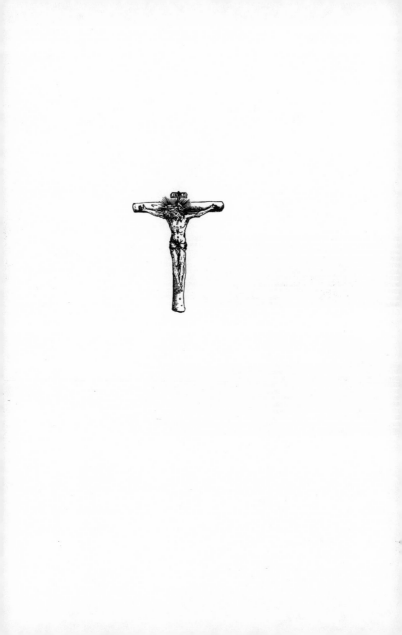

JOHANN GERHARD

MEDITATIONS
ON
DIVINE MERCY

A Classic Treasury of Devotional Prayers

TRANSLATED BY MATTHEW C. HARRISON

CONCORDIA PUBLISHING HOUSE · SAINT LOUIS

To all the faithful donors who give so generously to LCMS World Relief and Human Care.

"God is able to make all grace abound to you, so that having all sufficiency in all things at all times, you may abound in every good work."

2 CORINTHIANS 9:8

CONTENTS

TRANSLATOR'S PREFACE

The following quotation from Martin Luther grabbed my heart and soul. It has become an anchor and motivation for the vocation of mercy in Christ's name to which I am called professionally and to which each of us is called by virtue of our Baptism and our participation in the Sacrament of the Altar.

> *Your heart must go out in love and learn that this sacrament is a sacrament of love. As love and support are given you, you in turn must render love and support to Christ in his needy ones. You must feel with sorrow all the dishonor done to Christ in his holy Word, all the misery of Christendom, all the unjust suffering of the innocent, with which the world is everywhere filled to overflowing. You must fight, work, pray, and—if you cannot do more—have heartfelt sympathy.*[1]

The vocation of mercy challenges each of us, but it is a particular challenge to those who live on the mercy edge of the church's life, those who work for the church as pastors, teachers, lay leaders, etc. But we travel a well-worn path as we go about our vocation of mercy: We follow in the footsteps of our Savior, Jesus Christ. Where do we find the strength to "fight, work, and pray" for those in need? We find it in Christ Himself.

Souls animated by Christ, lives washed in the saving flood of Baptism, hearts forgiven by our Savior's body and blood—we can do nothing other than look with mercy on those who suffer. Moreover, our Lord Himself demonstrated for us how to show love and mercy toward those who are hurting in body and soul— He prayed for them. He also prayed for Himself so He would have strength for His ultimate task—to die for a world in need of mercy. Now Christ bids us—those who have been forgiven by virtue of His death and are dead to sin, death, and devil—to "fight, work, pray, and . . . have heartfelt sympathy."

It is for the "praying" in Luther's equation that this book is offered to you. In my personal life of prayer, I have found no greater tool—except the Bible—than these meditations on mercy by Johann Gerhard. This great pastor and teacher struggled under the cross. Plagued by illness, Christ blessed Dr. Gerhard with spiritual strength and insight at a remarkably young age. With great joy, I present these meditations to the church in English translation. It is my prayer that in them, dear reader, the stark message of the Law will drive you to the Savior's arms. It is my prayer that in His embrace you will bask in the sweet sunshine of the Gospel. Finally, I pray that as a church that has received mercy, we will be empowered and set aflame with passion to "fight, work, and pray" for the multitudes within and without the church who need Christ and His mercy.

Johann Gerhard is one of the three greatest classical Lutheran theologians. After Luther (1483–1546) and

Martin Chemnitz (1522–1586), "Gerhard (1582–1637) is the third after which there is no fourth." At a young age, Gerhard suffered severe depression and health difficulties. This experience, along with extensive study of the Bible and reading of the ancient theologians of the church, produced a deep piety in a gifted young man. Although he wrote extensive doctrinal treatises, Gerhard also produced several devotionals. This particular volume is Gerhard's *Exercitium Pietatis Quotidianum*[2] or *Daily Exercise of Piety,* which has been retitled *Meditations on Divine Mercy.* It was originally published in Coburg, Germany, in 1612 when Gerhard was 30 years old and already a seasoned leader of the church. The final 1629 edition was published in Jena, dedicated to Paul Heigel, and is the basis for this translation.

May these meditations on our merciful Lord make you ever more His merciful servant in love toward all who are in need.

Rev. Matthew C. Harrison
*Executive Director, LCMS World
    Relief and Human Care*
Easter III, 2003
1 John 3:16ff.

MEDITATIONS
ON
DIVINE MERCY

DEDICATION

To a distinguished man, with distinction,
piety, learning, and virtue of old,

Lord Paul Heigel of Polokowitz,

highly esteemed assessor of the harmo-
nious senate in renowned and imperial
Nuremberg, lord, patron, and especially
beloved and honored friend ... Receive from
me, most honorable man, this little paper
gift. Receive from my insignificance all reverence, all compliance, and every kind of
service expected in the future. May the Lord
Jesus graciously grant to you, noble and
highly esteemed friend, a long life and all
prosperity of soul and body. I have written
this at Jena, the first day of June, 1629.

From your noble and honorable,
most devoted

Johann Gerhard, Doctor[3]

WHAT IS PRAYER?

IF SOMEONE WANTS TO DESCRIBE adequately the usefulness of pious, earnest prayer, he will, in my opinion, surely find a beginning more easily than a conclusion. Pious prayer offered in faith is familiar conversation with God. It is a salutary remedy to all the difficulties of life. It is the key to heaven and the door to paradise. It shows us how much we depend on God, and it is a ladder of ascension to God. It is a shield for our defense and a faithful messenger of the ambassador. It is refreshment in the heat of misfortune; it is medicine during illness. It is a winch, drawing us to heaven, and a vessel that draws water from the font of divine kindness. It is a sword against the devil and a defense against misfortune. It is a wind that blows away evil and brings earthly benefits. It is a nurse that nurtures virtue and conquers faults. It is a great fortification for the soul and gives free access to God. It is a spiritual feast and a heavenly delicacy. It is a consolation for the dejected and a delight for the holy. It grants knowledge of the secret things of God and acquires His gifts. It upholds the world and rescues people. It is a joy for the heart and a jubilation for the mind. It follows God's gift of grace, and it leads ahead into glory. It is a garden of happiness and a tree full of delights. It calms the conscience and increases our thankfulness. It sends demons running and draws angels close. It is a soothing remedy for the misfortunes of this life and the sweet smell of the sacrifice of thanksgiving. It is a foretaste of the life to come and sweetens the bitterness of death.[4]

Whoever is truly a child of God through faith will, with childlike trust, address his or her heavenly Father every day in prayer. The one in whose heart the Holy Spirit has made His home will, as a spiritual priest, daily offer to God this incense of prayer. There are four immovable truths on which our confidence to pray rests. Because of these, we may be certain that our heavenly Father mercifully hears our prayers. The truths on which our certainty rests are: (1) God's omnipotent kindness; (2) God's unfailing truthfulness; (3) Christ's intercession as our mediator; and (4) the Holy Spirit's testimony.

GOD'S OMNIPOTENT KINDNESS

How much has God given to us without our asking? He has given us body and soul. He has even given us His own Son. What will He give to us if only we ask Him? Because God has given us such great things, we can have courage and confidence when we ask Him for lesser things. Everything we ask for is insignificant compared to the fact that the Son of God willingly suffered and died for us. God's goodness is boundless and infinite. What can He deny to us? The love by which we hold fast to God, no matter how faint it may be, makes us eagerly desire to be subject to God's will in all things. Even so, we are much more sure of God's boundless love and goodness. Is not this the trust God wants? "He fulfills the desire of those who fear Him" (Psalm 145:19), says the psalmist, doubtless because God shows those who fear Him the purest and most perfect love. Indeed, perfect love gives itself totally to the one who is loved and grants what he or she desires. God's goodness is omnipotent. Is there anything He cannot give to us? Nothing that God has promised is too hard or too difficult, much less impossible, for Him to do because He is the highest power (Luke 1:37).

GOD'S UNFAILING TRUTHFULNESS

God graciously promises us that He will listen intently when we pray. This promise is a word of eternal and immovable truth because God is truth itself (John 14:6). God cannot deny Himself or His word (2 Timothy 2:13). God promises that He will favorably hear our prayers. As if this were not enough, Christ also affirmed it by swearing an oath. He said to the apostles, and through them to anyone else who truly believes, "Truly, truly, I say to you, whatever you ask of the Father in My name, He will give it to you" (John 16:23). If you do not believe God the Father's promise, believe Christ, who swears the oath. "You have said, 'Seek My face.' My heart says to You, 'Your face, LORD, do I seek'" (Psalm 27:8).

CHRIST'S INTERCESSION
AS OUR MEDIATOR

The third truth that assures us that God favorably hears our prayers is Christ's intercession as our mediator. He is "at the right hand of God, who indeed is interceding for us" (Romans 8:34) and is our "advocate with the Father" (1 John 2:1). What will the heavenly Father deny to His beloved Son? What will our gracious Savior not obtain by the power and merit of His satisfaction accomplished for us? The shrine of heaven stands open to Him. Christ delivers our prayers to the secret council of God. Will the Father not hear Him? Will He refuse anything to Him? Will He not hear Himself? Will He refuse Himself anything? The Father and the Son "are one" (John 10:30). The Son is "at the Father's side" (John 1:18). And "the Father is in [Christ] and [Christ is] in the Father" (John 10:38; 14:10). Christ our intercessor says to the Father, "I knew that You always hear Me" (John 11:42). If Christ was heard by the Father while He walked the earth as God in the flesh, appearing in weakness in the state of humiliation (Philippians 2:7), the Father will certainly hear Christ now in His state of exultation (Philippians 4:10) as He rules in all the glory of His majesty and as He exercises the full measure of His power.

THE HOLY SPIRIT'S WORK

The fourth truth that assures us that God favorably hears our prayers is the testimony of the Holy Spirit. "You have received the Spirit of adoption as sons, by whom we cry, 'Abba! Father!' The Spirit Himself bears witness with our spirit that we are children of God" (Romans 8:15–16; Galatians 4:6). Surely God hears those groans, those wailings, those prayers, those sighs that the Holy Spirit works in us. If God did not, He would be despising and rejecting His own work. "Likewise the Spirit helps us in our weakness. For we do not know what to pray for as we ought, but the Spirit Himself intercedes for us with groanings too deep for words" (Romans 8:26). The Spirit does not intercede for us with human expressions. Instead, according to His nature, the Holy Spirit pours Himself over our prayers to cover our lack of skill and forethought with His working and presence. In this way, He requests from God that which is beneficial for us.

On these four truths our hearts rest confidently and securely so we will not waver in prayer nor doubt that God favorably hears our prayers. "Let us then with confidence draw near to the throne of grace, that we may receive mercy and find grace to help in time of need" (Hebrews 4:16). None of us should take our prayers lightly. God, to whom we pray, does not take them lightly. Before they pass over our lips, He commands them to be written in His book. We must hope, without doubt, for one of two things: Either our heavenly Father will give to us what we ask, or He will give to us that which He knows to be most beneficial for us.

Furthermore, anyone with a sound mind and good judgment, anyone who considers the divine majesty of God and our weakness, understands how profitable and necessary it is to pray without ceasing and how difficult it is to do (Luke 18:1; 1 Thessalonians 5:17). When you stand before the Lord to pray, stand before Him with great fear and desire. Break the chains of earthly anxiety from your heart. Fight courageously so your speech may be holy, pure, and unstained, and the gates of heaven will open before your prayer. The angels will meet it with joy and carry it to the throne of the blessed Father. Rather than being like those who tempt the Lord, we can prepare our hearts and come before God our Father in prayer (Sirach 18:23).

CONCERNING THE ARRANGEMENT
OF THIS BOOK

There are four parts to daily meditation:

1. We ask God to forgive our sins because of Christ.

2. We offer humble thanks to God for His blessings.

3. We pray that the Holy Spirit might preserve and increase His gifts to us by which He gives us spiritual victory over our temptations.

4. We pray for the needs of our neighbor, both for this life and for eternal life.

First, we consider our sin, the forgiveness of which is to be asked of God because of Christ. Second, we acknowledge the benefits we receive from God, for which humble thanksgiving is to be offered. Third, we consider our need and pray for the preservation and increase of the gifts of the Holy Spirit and for spiritual victory over all temptations. Fourth, we remember our neighbor's need and pray for those things that our neighbor needs for this life and for eternal life.

PART I

CONCERNING MEDITATION
ON SINS

MEDITATION ON SIN consists of two parts. First, we recognize the seriousness of original and actual sin. Actual sins are committed by thought, word, and deed. We sin when we do evil or fail to do good. We sin against God, our neighbor, and our self. There are sins of youth and of daily weaknesses. Every day we are tempted by the flesh, and we will often succumb to these temptations. At times we participate in the sins of others and fall into many of these same sins ourselves. Indeed, we are convicted of the guilt of our sins by all creation. Second, we contemplate the severity of divine wrath against our sins when we meditate on the suffering and death of Christ.

I

THE SERIOUSNESS
OF ORIGINAL SIN

O HOLY GOD, just Judge, I know that I am conceived and born in sin (Psalm 51:7). I know that I was formed from unclean seed in my mother's womb (Job 14:4). The poison of sin has so corrupted and spoiled my entire nature that no power of my soul is free from its infection. The holy gift of the divine image entrusted to me by the first parent of our race has perished in me. I now have no ability to initiate a saving recognition, fear, trust, and love of You. I have no ability to obey Your commandments. My will is turned away from the Law. The law of sin in my members is opposed to the law of my mind so my entire nature is corrupt and perverted (Romans 7:23). I am wretched and miserable. I feel the assault of sin clinging tenaciously to every part of me. I feel the yoke of perverse desire weighing heavily on me. Although I have been regenerated and renewed in the washing of Baptism through the Spirit of grace (Titus 3:5), I am not totally free from the yoke and captivity of sin. That bitter root lurking in me always strives to shoot forth (Hebrews 12:15). The law of sin that rages in my flesh fights to capture me. I am full of doubts and distrust. I desire my own honor. From my heart come depraved thoughts that defile me in Your sight (Matthew 15:19). From a poisoned spring flow poison streams.

O Lord, do not enter into judgment with Your servant (Psalm 143:2). Instead, be gracious to me according to Your great mercy (Psalm 51:3). The depth of my wretchedness calls out for help to the depth of Your mercy (Psalm 42:8). I place before You the holy conception of Your Son in place of my foul, unclean nature. He was born for me, and He also was conceived for me (Isaiah 9:6). Your Son was made sanctification and righteousness for me (1 Corinthians 1:30), and He also was made my purification and purity. Because of Your Son and through Your Son, have mercy on me, O Most High. Do not place the hidden, evil corruption of my nature in the light of Your face (Psalm 90:8). Look to Your beloved Son, my mediator. May His most holy and unpolluted conception be the remedy for my miserable conception.

AMEN.

II

REMEMBERING THE SINS
OF YOUTH

O HOLY GOD, just Judge, do not remember the faults of
my youth (Psalm 25:7). Do not recall any more the sins
of my past (Jeremiah 31:34). The root of evil desire produced so much poison fruit in my childhood. The evil
of original sin produced so many actual sins. The
thoughts of my heart are depraved and perverse from
earliest childhood, even from tender infancy (Genesis
6:5). If I were a day-old infant, in Your sight I would still
not be innocent (Job 14:4). The faults and failures that
weigh on me are as many as the days of my life; in fact,
they are many more because even a righteous person
falls seven times in a day (Proverbs 24:16). If a righteous
person falls seven times in a day, I believe that I, hope-
less and unrighteous, have fallen seventy times seven
times in a day.

Life increased and the web of sins increased.
However much You kindly added to the length of my
life, my defective and corrupt nature added an equal
amount to the weight of my sins. I look back at my life
and find the most foul and filthy cloak of sins. When I
compare the course of my life to the light of Your pre-
cepts, I find only darkness and blindness. My youth

should have been picked like a tender young flower, worn as a crown of virtue, and offered to You as a fragrant scent. The best of my years should have belonged to You, the Creator of nature. But the filth of sins polluted that flower of my youth in the foulest way. The stinking filth of transgressions fouled it terribly and miserably. Of all our years, the earliest are the most apt time for us to serve God. However, I used most of mine to serve the devil. The memory of many sins committed in my promiscuous and uncontrolled youth weighs heavy on my mind. Worse yet, many more of these sins escape my memory. Who can discern his errors? Forgive my hidden faults (Psalm 19:12).

For the disobedience of my youth, I offer to You, holy Father, the obedience of Your Son. I offer to You the perfect innocence of the one who became obedient to You, even to death, even death on a cross (Philippians 2:8). Even as a boy of twelve, Christ showed a holy obedience to You and followed Your will with great willingness (Luke 2:42). This obedience, O just Judge, I offer as the price and satisfaction for the great disobedience of my youth.

AMEN.

III

THE DAILY LAPSE
INTO SIN

O HOLY GOD, just Judge, no one is innocent in Your sight. No one is free from the uncleanliness of sin (Job 14:4). I do not possess that glory that I must bring with me when I stand before Your throne of judgment (Romans 3:23). I do not have the robe of innocence in which I must be clothed in Your sight. Seven times, no, many more times in every hour I fail (Proverbs 24:16). Every day I sin seventy times seven times. The spirit is sometimes willing, but the flesh is always weak (Matthew 26:41). The inner man is at times strong and firm, but the outer man is faint and weak. I do not do the good that I want to do, but I do the evil that I do not want to do (Romans 7:19). Depraved and impious thoughts appear in my mind. Vain, useless, and harmful words come out of my mouth. Perverse, depraved, and unbefitting deeds pollute me. All my righteous deeds are as filthy rags (Isaiah 64:6).

I do not dare to assert my righteousness before You (Romans 10:3). Instead, I deeply humble myself before Your most righteous tribunal. I cry out to You from the depths (Psalm 130:1, 3). Lord, if You hold our sins against us, who will survive? If You enter into judgment against

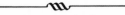

us, who will remain (Psalm 143:2)? If You measure us by the severe examination Your righteousness demands, how will we be able to stand before You? If You require an exact accounting for my life, I cannot give an excuse either for a thousand sins or for one (Job 9:3). My mouth is stopped (Romans 3:19). I confess that before You I am worthy of eternal suffering. I tearfully confess that I justly deserve eternal imprisonment.

For these sins that I commit every day of my life, I offer to You, O holy Father, the precious blood of Your Son, which was poured out on the altar of the cross. His blood cleanses me from all my transgressions (1 John 1:7). My sins hold me captive and are powerful enemies, but still more precious and efficacious is the ransom of Your Son. May that most perfect, full, and holy ransom of Christ avail for me, for the forgiveness of my transgressions.

AMEN.

IV

LIFE CONTEMPLATED ACCORDING TO THE FIRST TABLE OF THE LAW

O HOLY GOD, just Judge, You gave to us Your Law on Mount Sinai (Exodus 20:1). You desired that it be the norm for all our actions, words, and thoughts. Thus whatever does not agree with this norm is considered sin in Your judgment (1 John 2:3; 3:4). Whenever I look into that brilliant mirror, I see my foulness, and I tremble violently. I ought to love You, God, above all things. But I often love the world and become oblivious to loving You (1 John 2:15). I ought to fear You, God, above all things. But I often sin willingly and forget to fear You. You require that I trust in You, my God, above all things. But in difficult situations my heart often wavers, and I nervously and anxiously doubt Your fatherly care. I ought to obey You, my God, with my whole heart. But my stubborn flesh often opposes my intention to obey and takes me prisoner, a captive to sin (Romans 7:23). My thoughts ought to be holy, my desires holy and pure. But often the glory of a quiet mind is disturbed by conceited and impious thoughts.

I ought to call on You, my God, with my whole heart. But my mind often wanders while praying and is anxiously troubled, wondering if my prayers are heard. How negligent I am in prayer and how feeble in trust. How often indeed my tongue prays, but I do not worship You in spirit and truth (John 4:23). How often I completely forget the kindness You show me. Every day You lavishly pour out Your gifts on me, but I do not pour forth thanks to You. How cold are my thoughts concerning the vast and countless gifts You have given to me. How incredibly feeble the devotion of my heart. I use Your gifts but do not praise You, their giver. I am stuck in the streams; I do not hasten to the source. Your Word is the Spirit's word of life (John 6:63), but I often hinder it from bringing forth fruit (Matthew 13:7). I ruin the work of the Holy Spirit in me. More often than not I snuff out the spark of good intention. I do not anxiously ask for the increase of Your gifts.

For this and all my sins and failures, I offer to You, my God, the faultless and perfect obedience of Your Son, who, in the days of His flesh, loved You perfectly with His whole heart and depended completely on You. No taint of sin was found in His deeds, words, and thoughts (Isaiah 53:9), not even the slightest stain of guilt. That which I lack, I confidently draw from His rich supply. Because of Your beloved Son, have mercy on me, Your servant, O Lord.

AMEN.

V

LIFE CONTEMPLATED ACCORDING TO THE SECOND TABLE OF THE LAW

O HOLY GOD, just Judge, it is Your eternal and unchangeable will that I truly honor my parents and other authorities (Exodus 20:12). But how often I give little consideration to their authority. I refuse to give them true obedience from the heart. I ridicule their weaknesses. I do not earnestly pray that You would preserve and keep them. I harbor anger against those to whom I ought to submit myself completely and patiently. Your holy will demands that, as much as I am able, I serve my neighbor in all things. But how often I weary of being kind or am seized by disdain for neighborly giving. How often my flesh rouses me to anger, hatred, jealousy, and contention. How often the fire of an angry heart burns within me, even if combative words are not heard on the outside. Your holy will requires that I live chastely, modestly, and in moderation. But how often the love of drunkenness and promiscuity make my soul captive to sin. How often the flames of passion seethe internally, even if the outer members are held in restraint. Jesus speaks the truth: "Everyone who looks at a woman with lustful intent has already committed adultery with her in his heart" (Matthew 5:28). How often, therefore, do we commit adultery according to God's judgment? The unwarranted and immoderate use of food, drink, and sex often creeps up on us unawares. It renders us guilty before You, O God, if You desire to enter into judgment with us. Your holy will demands that I in no way cheat my neighbor in matters of business, but that I seek my neighbor's advantage. I am in no way to ridicule my neighbor's faults; instead, I am to cover them with the mantle of love. I am not to accuse my neighbor with a quick and rash judgment. But how often I seek my own advantage through unjust means. How often I make a rash judgment concerning my neighbor. Your holy will demands that my spirit, mind, and soul be free from every depraved desire. But how often my flesh incites me to sin and how often perverse desires pollute my spirit. Like a spring continually overflows with gushing water, my heart boils continually with depraved desires (Jeremiah 6:7).

For these and all my sins and failures, I offer to You, most holy Father, the perfect obedience of Your Son, who loved all people with perfect love. In His mouth was found no deceit (Isaiah 53:9; 1 Peter 2:22). He did not deviate from Your Law in His words or deeds. There was no corruption in His nature. To this mercy seat I flee in true faith (Exodus 25:17; Romans 3:25; Hebrews 9:5). Through faith, I draw from His wounds everything that is necessary for righteousness and salvation. Have mercy on me, my God and my Father.

AMEN.

VI

PARTICIPATION
IN THE SINS OF OTHERS

O HOLY GOD, just Judge, You have committed to me not only the care of my own soul, but also the care of my neighbor's. But how often my carelessness causes great detriment to my neighbor's piety. How often I fail to rebuke my neighbor frankly and forthrightly for sin. How often I accuse my neighbor less forthrightly of faults, held back by fear or by a desire for my neighbor's favor. I am lax in praying for my neighbor's salvation (1 Timothy 2:1). I am timid in rebuking my neighbor for sin (Ezekiel 3:21). I am faint in the advancement of my neighbor's salvation. Thus You most righteously are able to hold me responsible for the blood of my perishing neighbor.

If my love for my neighbor were perfect and sincere, then that love would surely produce a candid and honest rebuke. If the fire of sincere love burned in my heart, then certainly it would flame more brightly as I offer the spiritual incense of prayer for my neighbor's salvation. We pray for ourselves all the time because we always are concerned for ourselves. But to ask God for the salvation of a neighbor is a work of love. When I do not pray for the salvation of my neighbor, I condemn myself by a violation of the law of love.

My neighbor dies a physical death, and I mourn and groan day and night, though physical death brings no harm to the godly person because it provides a transition to the heavenly kingdom. My neighbor dies a spiritual death by committing mortal sins, and I watch my neighbor die without concern. I am not grieved at all, though sin is the true death of the soul through which comes the inestimable loss of divine grace and eternal life. My neighbor offends the king, and I seek my neighbor's reconciliation by every means available. My neighbor offends the King of kings, who is able to dispatch soul and body to hell (Matthew 10:28), and I look on without concern. I do not consider this offense of the King to be an immeasurable evil. My neighbor stumbles on a stone, and I quickly prevent the fall or help my neighbor up from the fall. My neighbor stumbles at the Cornerstone of our salvation (Psalm 118:22), and I show careless neglect. Void of the concern and attentiveness I ought to have, I do not lift up my neighbor again. My sins are many and weighty enough, but still I am not afraid to participate in someone else's sins.

Be gracious, O God. I am a great and immeasurably burdened sinner. I carry my sins and the sins of others. I flee to Your mercy, which is promised to me in and through Christ. I, who am dead in sin, draw near to the Life (John 14:6). I, who am erring in the way of sin, draw near to the Way. I, who because of sin am worthy of damnation, draw near to the Salvation. Make me alive. Direct and save me for eternity, my true Life, Way, and Salvation.

AMEN.

VII

ALL CREATION
CONVICTS US OF SIN

O HOLY GOD, just Judge, if I look toward heaven, I remember that You, my God, are offended by me in many ways. I have sinned, Father, against heaven and before You. I am not worthy to be called Your child (Luke 15:18). If I look toward earth, I realize that through my sin I have disgracefully wasted creation. I have often wasted not only the darkness of night, but also the light of day as I go about my works of darkness. If I consider the example of those sinners whom You have punished by Your just judgment, I find that my sins are as weighty as theirs. If I consider the example of the saints, I find that I am entirely unequal to their diligent service to You. If I consider my guardian angel, I find that my sin has often put him to flight. If I consider the devil, I find that often I have given in to his suggestions. If I weigh carefully the sternness of Your Law, I find that in so many ways my life does not measure up to its demands. If I consider my conscience, I find that the thoughts of my mind accuse me as I face Your judgment. If I consider the approaching hour of death, I realize that it is the just reward for my sins (Romans 6:23). If You were not to receive me out of pure mercy because of Christ, my death would be the entrance to and beginning of eternal death. If I consider the coming judgment, I find that I fully deserve that my sins be avenged with strictest severity. My sins deserve to be subjected to the most exact calculation of divine justice. If I consider hell, I find that because of my sins, I have rightly merited its punishments. If I consider eternal life, I find that because of my sins I have justly and rightly lost the hope of attaining it. Therefore, all my sins convict me. Please, God, do not turn to me in harshness!

I flee to Christ, Your beloved Son, my only mediator. Through Christ, I believe without any doubt that Your grace and the forgiveness of sins apply to me. All creation accuses me. My conscience accuses me. Both tables of the divine Law accuse me. Day and night Satan accuses me. But You, O kindest Jesus, take up my defense. The poor person is left to You (Psalm 10:14). You desire that I forsake comfort in any created thing. A refuge has been prepared for me in the satisfaction You made for my sins. I have a refuge in Your intercession for me at the right hand of the Father. Take flight, O my soul, to the morning light. Like a dove, hide in the clefts of the rock (Song of Songs 2:14), take refuge in the wounds of Christ, your Savior. Hide in this rock until the wrath of the Lord passes by, and you will find rest in this refuge. You will find protection. You will find acquittal.

AMEN.

VIII

CONTRITION CONVINCES US OF THE SERIOUSNESS OF SIN

O HOLY GOD, just Judge, my heart is contrite and humble. My spirit is sad and afflicted because of my sins (Isaiah 66:2). I am overwhelmed with anxiety and weighed down. I've lost all my courage, and my eyes are dark with depression. I am overwhelmed, and I begin to weep. My spirit is full of anxiety, and I forget to eat. My heart is wounded, and a fountain of tears pours forth, the blood of a wounded heart. Who can discern one's errors (Psalm 19:13)? Who understands the pain of the heart surrounded by failures and faults? My parched and contrite soul thirsts for You, the font of life (Psalm 42:2). O Christ, nourish me with the dew of the Spirit and of grace. My anguished heart groans for You. O true Joy, give to me peace and quiet of conscience (Psalm 51:10) so, justified by faith, I might have peace with God (Romans 5:1).

My heart condemns me, but You, who are stronger than my heart, absolve me (1 John 3:20). My conscience accuses me, but You, who affixed the handwriting of conscience to the cross, acquit me (Colossians

2:14). I offer to You, my God, my contrite and humbled heart as a most grateful sacrifice (Psalm 51:19). I offer to You my groans, messengers of true and real sorrow over sin. I offer to You my tears, abundant witnesses of earnest sorrow. I despair of myself. In You, hope is repaired. Of myself, I fail. In You, I am restored. In me, there is anguish. In You, I find joy once again. I am weary and heavy laden (Matthew 11:28). You restore me and give rest to my soul. The deep calls out to the deep (Psalm 42:7). The depth of my misery calls out to the depth of Your mercy. From the depths I cry out to You (Psalm 130:1). Cast my sins into the depths of the sea (Micah 7:19). There is no soundness in my flesh because of Your wrath (Psalm 38:3). There is no peace in my bones because of my sin. My sins overwhelm me. They are like a great weight that becomes ever more burdensome as it is carried.

Heal my soul, O heavenly Physician, or death will swallow me. Take the weight of sins away from me, You who bore that weight on the cross, or I will lose hope under this unbearable burden. Have mercy on me, Font of grace and mercy.

AMEN.

IX

GOD'S DEEDS OF KINDNESS TESTIFY TO THE GRAVITY OF SIN

O HOLY GOD, just Judge, the more deeds of kindness You give to me, the more I am grieved that I have so often offended You, my benevolent Father. Every gift You have given to me is like a bond of love. You have willed that I be bound to You, but I heap up the number of sins because I forget about You and Your kindness. I have sinned, Father, against heaven and before You. I am not worthy to be called Your child. Make me as one of Your hired servants (Luke 15:19). I am totally dissatisfied with myself. Grant that I would be totally pleasing to You. The riches of Your goodness and Your extraordinary patience (Romans 2:4) have, for a long time, called me to repentance, but so far I have declined to come. O most benevolent Father, again and again You have called me to repentance through the preaching of the Word, through the admonition of creation, through the reproof shown Christ on the cross, through the internal working of the Holy Spirit, but I have completely closed my ears to this calling.

All the powers of my soul, all the members of my body, are Your gifts. I should be prepared to offer You the holy service I owe to You with all the power of my soul and with all the members of my body. But what cause for sorrow!—I have made them tools for unrighteousness and evil. Yours is the breath that I draw. Yours is the air that I breathe. Yours is the sun whose light I behold every day. All these should be aids and tools for a holy life. But what sorrow!—I have turned them into servants of sin. Creation is to be used for the glory of the Creator, but unfortunately I have misused it for His dishonor. The armor of light is to be put on in the light of the sun, but in the sun's light, I have committed works of darkness (Romans 13:12). Whatever time is added to my life is given to me because of Your kindness. Therefore, my whole life should be devoted to You, the one from whom everything comes. But not even the smallest part of my life is devoted to You in holy service. I often sense what is good and right to do, but I often fail to follow through and I turn away from service to You. The good impulses invite me to return to You through repentance, but I often harshly shun their loving encouragement.

Receive the one who now at last returns to You with groaning and a contrite heart. Sprinkle me with the blood of Your Son so I may be cleansed whiter than snow (Psalm 51:7) from all the filthiness of my flesh and spirit (2 Corinthians 7:1). May I praise You eternally with all the elect.

AMEN.

X

THE SEVERITY OF DIVINE WRATH AGAINST SIN CONSIDERED IN THE PASSION AND DEATH OF CHRIST

O HOLY GOD, just Judge, I see Your Son hanging on the cross, streams of blood flowing freely. I look at Him and, behold, I become weak with terror. Those cruel nails are my sins with which I have pierced His hands and feet. Those horrible thorns are my sins with which I have crowned His holy head, the head worshiped and honored by angelic powers. Those sharply pointed lashes are my sins with which I have scourged His faultless body, the permanent temple of divinity. A terrible beast tore to pieces this heavenly Joseph and stained His robe with blood (Genesis 37:33). I, a wretched sinner, am that terrible beast because my sins rushed en masse against this Your beloved Son (Isaiah 53:6).

If this, Your obedient Son, suffers in anguish because of the sins of another, what will be meted out to disobedient and wayward children because of their sins? Truly, the wounds of my soul must be great and deadly if they can only be healed because Your only begotten Son is so wretchedly struck down. Truly, the disease of my soul must be great and deadly if it can only be cured because the heavenly Physician, Life itself, dies on a cross.

I see the torment of my Savior. I hear His wretched wailings on the cross (Matthew 27:46). He is tormented because of me. He complains loudly that His Father has forsaken Him because of my sins. If the weight of another's sins strikes down the all-powerful Son of God, how unbearable will the wrath of God and His inestimable furor be against the unprofitable servant (Luke 17:10)? O dry and unfruitful wood, sold to the fires of eternal hell, what will be your lot if this is what happens to the green wood (Luke 23:31)? Christ is the green tree of life. Christ is a vigorous tree, rooted in divinity, part and parcel of humanity, famed for His virtues, possessing leaves of holy words, and yielding the fruit of good works. He is the cedar of modesty and the vine of peace, the palm of patience and the olive of mercy.

But if the fire of divine wrath burned against this green wood, the tree of life, because of the sins of others, how much more will it completely consume the sinner as a dry tree because of unfruitful works? How great and bloody the letters of my sin appear when written on the body of Christ. How striking, O most righteous God, is Your wrath against my iniquity. How tightly I must have been held in captivity because so precious a ransom was given to release me. How great the stains of my sin must have been because streams of blood from the body of Christ flowed to wash them away (Luke 22:44).

O most righteous God, yet most kind Father, behold how unworthily Your Son suffered for me. Forget how unworthily I, Your wretched servant, have acted. Look to Christ's deep wounds and plunge my sins into the deepest depths of the sea of Your mercy (Micah 7:19).

AMEN.

PART II

CONCERNING MEDITATION
ON GOD'S GIFTS

THE CONTEMPLATION OF GOD'S GIFTS from the most beautiful garden of nature and the church is like gathering a bouquet of fragrant flowers. The scent of these blooms refreshes the spirit and calls forth the sacrifice of praise, which is a sweet smell to God. These immeasurable and countless divine gifts may be considered according to the three articles of the Christian faith. God has created, redeemed, and sanctified us. He showers us in this life with the greatest gifts. He promises even more for eternal life. He gives us gifts for the care of soul, body, and external needs. He guards us from evil and preserves us in the good. He conceals what has happened in the past. He controls what will happen in the future. Even as He has bestowed many past blessings of grace, still more are the blessings He gives that protect us from evil. In short, we can grasp neither in word nor in thought the number and worth of those divine gifts that will be the most abundant subject of eternal praise in the coming life.

I

THANKSGIVING
FOR LIFE
AND BIRTH

OMNIPOTENT, ETERNAL GOD, Father, Son, and Holy
Spirit, I give You thanks. I praise You. I glorify You
because Your hands fashioned me and made every
detail of what I am. You shaped me like clay in my
mother's womb. You poured me out like milk and cur-
dled me like cheese. You clothed me with skin and knit
me together with bones and tendons. You gave me life
and showed me mercy. In Your providence, You
watched over my spirit (Job 10:9–12).

I will celebrate the great mercy You have shown
me with eternal praises. Your kindness I will declare
with everlasting songs of praise. You covered me in my
mother's womb. I will praise You because I am wonderfully made. Marvelous are Your works, which my soul
knows well. My frame was not hidden from You because
You made me in secret when You adorned me with my
various members in the lower parts of the earth. Your
eyes saw me when I was yet unformed. In Your book
were written all the days that would be, though not yet
one of them was.

How precious are Your thoughts to me, O God. How great is their sum. If I were to count them, they would be more in number than the sands of the sea (Psalm 139:13–18). You showed Your mercy before I could perceive it. You came to me with Your kindness before I could long for it. Your generosity encompassed me before I could offer thanks for it. You not only marvelously formed me in my mother's womb, but also drew me out from the womb. You have been my hope since I was at my mother's breast. I was cast on You from birth. From my mother's womb, You have been my God (Psalm 22:10–11).

When I consider how many die in the womb before coming to the light of this life, I admire and praise Your mercy all the more because You brought me—alive, safe and sound—out of the confinement of the womb into the theater of this world. How many years passed in which I was nothing. But it pleased You to build this dwelling of my body and to bring it out of the deep darkness of my mother's womb. You have given me a rational soul and did not will that I be a stone or a snake. To You, my God, be honor and glory forever for this, Your mercy.

AMEN.

II

THANKSGIVING FOR PRESERVATION

OMNIPOTENT, MERCIFUL GOD, I thank You for wonderfully preserving me from the earliest days of my life. I came into this world naked (1 Timothy 6:7). You kindly clothed me. I entered this world hungry. Thus far You generously have fed me. In You, I live and move (Acts 17:28). Without You, I fall back to nothing and die. In You, I bend and move my limbs. Without You, I cannot participate in life and movement. The sun that provides me light, which I see daily with my eyes, belongs to You (Psalm 104:2; Matthew 5:45). The air that I continually breathe belongs to You. The day belongs to You. The night belongs to You. The alternation of day and night provides me opportunity for labor and rest. The earth whose fruit generously nourishes me belongs to You. Every creature in heaven, sky, land, and sea that is designated for my use and service is Yours. Silver is Yours. Gold is Yours (Haggai 2:8). For whatever is necessary for the preservation of this life, I have Your most generous and kind hands to thank.

How generous You are to the whole human race, O God. You created all things for our use. You preserve all things for our sake. Whatever You provide for creation, You provide for me because for my sake You wonderfully formed, established, and preserved all these things. Some creatures serve us by obedience. Some serve for nourishment, some for clothing, some for healing, some for punishment. All creatures teach and instruct us. Who can number the types of food that You have created and that You continue to produce from the earth to feed us? Who can count the species of herbs that You call forth from the earth each year for our healing? Who can describe the animals created for our use and for our service?

To You, the creator and preserver of all things, be glory and honor forever. Without You, the true sun, I would vanish like a shadow. Without You, the true light, I would be destroyed immediately. Without You, the true being, I would be brought to nothing instantly. To You alone do I owe my being, my living, and my moving. Therefore, I will live only for You and depend only on You for eternity.

AMEN.

III

THANKSGIVING
FOR
REDEMPTION
THROUGH CHRIST

ETERNAL, OMNIPOTENT GOD, I give to You the greatest thanks because You created me when I was nothing. I thank You much more because You redeemed me when I was lost and condemned, caught in the jaws of hell. But You removed me by the blood of Your Son (Colossians 1:14). I was a slave to Satan. But by Your grace, You freed me from the dominion of the devil and placed me in the kingdom of Christ. I am entirely indebted to You because You formed me in my entirety. I am obliged to praise You with my tongue because You gave it to me (Psalm 51:15). My mouth is obliged to announce Your praise because it breathes the air and breath You provide. My heart is obliged to cling to You with continual love because You formed it. All my members are obliged to serve You quickly because, however many and great they are, You wondrously made them all.

If I am already indebted to You because You have made me, what can I possibly give back to You for my redemption from servitude and captivity to sin? You have rescued the lost sheep from the claws of the infernal wolf (John 10:28). You have freed the runaway slave from the prison of the devil. You have anxiously sought the lost coin (Luke 15:8). In Adam, I fell. You raised me up. In Adam, I was held captive by the chains of sin. You broke those chains. In Adam, I perished. You desired to save me again. Who am I, miserable worm, that You were so anxious for my redemption and desired to do so much for my salvation? If the parents of our race were utterly rejected by You after the fall, and they, together with all their descendants, were removed from the sight of Your glory and cast into the deepest hell, not one of us could complain of injustice. We receive what our deeds deserve. What else could we ask or expect from You, who created us in Your image and provided us with sufficient power to guard our innocence?

You showed Your incomprehensible and unspeakably great love toward us when You promised a Son, a Savior, to the first parents after the fall (Genesis 3:15). In the fullness of time, You sent this Savior to us. Through Him, You recall us from death to life, from sin to righteousness, from hell to heavenly glory. O Lover of all humanity, whose delight is in the children of men (Proverbs 8:31), who can offer worthy praise for this philanthropy? Moreover, who can conceive of it? These are the incomprehensible riches of Your goodness. This is the immeasurable treasure of Your kindness, which our impoverished understanding cannot grasp. The slaves were so valuable that for their redemption the Son was given up to death. The one hostile to You was so loved that You appointed the beloved Son to be my Redeemer. My soul is astounded as I reflect on this kindness. It is deeply moved and melts in love for You.

AMEN.

IV

THANKSGIVING
FOR
CHRIST'S INCARNATION

JESUS CHRIST, only mediator and redeemer of the human race, I give thanks to You that in the fullness of time You united Yourself personally to a true human nature and deigned to be born of a virgin (Galatians 4:4). How great is Your love for Your human creatures that You laid hold not of angels, but of the seed of Abraham (Hebrews 2:16). How great is the mystery of godliness that You, being true God, desired to become manifest in the flesh (1 Timothy 3:16). How great is Your mercy that, descending from heaven for my sake, You endured being born of a virgin (Isaiah 9:6). For me, a most worthless creature, You, the all-powerful Creator, became man. For my sake, an abject slave, You, the glorious Lord, clothed Yourself in servile fashion with a body so with flesh You might free flesh (Philippians 2:7). For me, You were born. Therefore, whatever heavenly goods You bring with You in Your birth will be mine.

Because You were given to me, so also shall all things be given to me. My nature is glorified more in

You than it was disgraced in Adam through sin. Because You assumed into the unity of Your person that which was only tarnished by Satan, You truly are flesh of my flesh and bone of my bone (Ephesians 5:30)].[5] You are my brother. What can you deny to me, the person to whom You are most intimately joined by the same essence of flesh and by the feeling of fraternal love? You are the bridegroom (Matthew 22:2) who, according to the good pleasure of the heavenly Father, bound the human nature to Yourself as a bride by means of a personal covenant. With a thankful soul, I proclaim and acknowledge that I, too, am invited to the celebration of this marriage.

I am no longer amazed that heaven, earth, sea, and all that is in them were made by God for us because God Himself ordained to become a man for the sake of His human creatures. Truly, You cannot reject me and turn me away because You cannot deny that You Yourself are a man and therefore my brother (2 Timothy 2:13). You can never forget me because You have engraved me on the palms of Your hands (Isaiah 49:16). Christ's communion with humanity daily and continually makes You mindful of me. You cannot forsake me because You, by the closest bond of the personal union, ordained to join the human nature to Yourself. Therefore, no matter how much my sins hinder me from coming to You for mercy, the communion of the two natures in Christ will not allow me to be driven away. I will depend totally on You, the one who totally assumed my humanity.

AMEN.

V

THANKSGIVING
FOR
CHRIST'S SUFFERING

O MOST GODLY JESUS, I thank You that, receiving the penalty of my sin, You willingly underwent hunger, thirst, cold, exhaustion, ridicule, persecution, sorrow, poverty, imprisonment, scourging, the piercing of thorns, and even a bitter death on a cross. How great is the fire of Your love that persuaded You to plunge willingly into the sea of that suffering for a miserable and ungrateful slave. In Your innocence and righteousness, You were free from all suffering, but Your immeasurable and indescribable love made You a debtor and a defendant in my place. I committed the crime; You underwent the punishment. I plundered; You made amends (Psalm 69:4). I sinned; You were punished.

O kindest Jesus, I recognize the depth of Your mercy and the earnestness of Your love (Luke 1:78). You appear to love me more than You love Yourself because You gave Yourself up for me. Why was the sentence of death pronounced on You? You are completely innocent. Why were You, the fairest among the sons of men, spit on (Psalm 45:2)? Why did You, the righteous one, undergo flogging and fetters? All these abuses rightly belonged to me. But You, because of unspeakable love, descended to the prison of this world. You clothed Yourself with my servile dwelling, willingly taking on Yourself what I justly deserve. Because of my sin, I was to be assigned to the unceasing, scorching flames of hell. But You boiled with the fire of love on the altar of the cross, setting me free from these flames. I was to be cast away from the face of the heavenly Father because of my sin. But for my sake, You chose to be abandoned by Your heavenly Father. I was to be tormented forever by the devil and his angels. But You, because of immeasurable love, gave Yourself for me and were harassed and crucified by the servants of Satan.

In the various ways You were made to suffer, I see evidence of Your love for me. Those fetters, those scourgings, those thorns that injured You were because of my sins. You bore all this because of me, because of Your indescribable love. Your love was not satisfied by the assumption of my flesh. You desired to establish that love even more firmly through that most bitter passion of Your soul and body. Who am I, most powerful Lord, that for the sake of a disobedient slave You willingly served so many years? Who am I, the most disgraceful bond-servant of sin and whore of the devil, that for my sake You, fairest bridegroom, did not refuse to die? Who am I, kindest Creator, that for my sake, a most wretched creature, You did not shrink from the punishment of the cross?

Truly, most loving Bridegroom, to You I am a blood bride. For my sake, You poured forth blood so abundantly. Truly, fairest Lily, to You I am an injurious and piercing thorn. I placed on You a harsh and enduring load. The weight of this so pressed You that drops of blood freely flowed from Your body. Because of Your love, Lord Jesus, only redeemer and mediator, I will sing psalms of praise to You for eternity.

AMEN.

VI

THANKSGIVING
FOR THE CALLING
THROUGH THE WORD

O LORD, MY GOD, I owe You praise, honor, and thanksgiving. You ordained to make known to us Your fatherly good pleasure and council concerning our salvation through the preaching of the Word. By nature, we are darkness (Ephesians 5:8). We sit in darkness and in the shadow of death (Luke 1:79). You dispel that darkness by the bright light of the Gospel. In Your light, we see light (Psalm 39:10). That is, in the light of Your Word, we see that true Light coming into the world that illumines all people (John 1:9). What good is a treasure concealed or a light hidden under a bushel (Matthew 5:15)? With a grateful soul, therefore, I proclaim Your vast kindness, that through the word of the Gospel You have revealed to us the treasure of the benefits of Your Son. How beautiful are the feet of those who proclaim Good News of good things and preach salvation (Isaiah 52:7; Nahum 1:15; Romans 10:15).

Today, You continue to announce this peace of conscience and salvation of the soul to us through the word of the Gospel. You call us to the kingdom of Your Son.

Like a pitiful, weak sheep, I was led astray, led into the way of error. You called me back to the right path through the Word. I was condemned and lost, but in the word of the Gospel, You brought to me the favor of Christ. In the favor of Christ, You brought me Your grace. In Your grace, You brought me the remission of sins. In the remission of sins, You brought me righteousness. In righteousness, You brought me eternal life and salvation. Who can proclaim the depth of Your mercy with words that are worthy enough? Who can even conceive of the magnitude and riches of Your kindness?

You have revealed to us through the manifestation of the Gospel the mystery of our salvation, which has been kept secret from eternity (Romans 16:25–26). Through the preaching of the Word, You reveal to us Your thoughts of peace concerning us, which You have had since before the foundation of the world (Jeremiah 29:11). This Word is a light to the feet of those who are striving through this dark vale for the eternal light (Psalm 119:105). What good would it have been for us to be born if You would not have freed us through Christ from the captivity of sin? What good would it have been to be redeemed if You would not have announced to us through the Word the immeasurable benefit of redemption? You stretch out Your hands to us all day (Isaiah 65:2). You knock at the door of our heart every day (Revelation 3:20), and through Your Word, You call all of us to Yourself, most gracious Lord.

Thousands and thousands live in the blindness of paganism and error. On them never falls as much of the light of the heavenly Word that You have granted to us, by Your goodness, though we are incredibly ungrateful. How often we deserve that You take from us the candle of the Word because of our ingratitude and contempt (Revelation 2:5). But You are patient and ignore our sin (Wisdom of Solomon 11:23). Because of unspeakable mercy, You preserve for us the holy deposit of the Word, the most valuable treasure. We give eternal thanks to You for this treasure. We humbly pray that You would continue to preserve this treasure among us.

AMEN.

VII

THANKSGIVING THAT GOD WAITS FOR OUR CONVERSION

MOST MERCIFUL FATHER, I give You eternal thanks because You waited for my conversion with such long-suffering patience and kindness (Romans 2:4) and that You led me from the path of sin to participation in Your kingdom. How great is Your long-suffering patience that You postponed a thousand times that which I justly deserved, namely, to be cast away from Your presence and into eternal punishment. How many thousands of people does death prevent from coming to true repentance? How many sinners has the devil hardened and kept from receiving the forgiveness of their sins? By nature, I am the same. The only thing that separates me from them is Your patient kindness and abounding grace, not any lesser guilt on my part.

Your mercy fought with my misery. I continued to sin. You continued to show mercy. I put off conversion. You put off administering the punishment I rightfully deserved. I wandered away, but You called me. I refused to come, but You waited for me. Most generous Father, I cannot praise Your kindness with accolades worthy enough. Kindest Father, I cannot repay You for Your long-suffering patience with any merit of my own. You guard me from committing innumerable sins. The corruption of the flesh, the seduction of the world, and the persuasion of the devil induce me to commit these sins, as they also induce others to sin. Not only do You keep and guard me so I do not fall into sins, You also wait kindly for me to turn away from those into which I have fallen. Your kindness surpasses my guilt. I sin, but You overlook it. I do not hold back from acting wickedly, but You hold back from whipping me. I greatly prolong my iniquity, but You delay rendering the punishment I justly deserve.

What then are my merits? Nothing but evil, yes, even the worst kind of evil. My merits are sins, in number most numerous, in weight most ponderous, in variety most abominable. I give credit to Your grace and kindness alone that You waited for my conversion with such patience and rescued my soul from the deathtrap of sin. To You, O Lord, be praise, honor, and glory forever.

AMEN.

VIII

THANKSGIVING
FOR
CONVERSION

O GRACIOUS GOD, I give thanks to You that You converted my hardened heart, which did not know how to repent, and that You removed my heart of stone and gave me a heart of flesh (Ezekiel 36:26). I had the power to fall into sin and guilt. I did not have the power to rise to repentance. By my own power, I was able to go astray. I was able to return to the right path only by Your power. Just as one who is born crippled cannot be restored with natural remedies but only by divine power, so my soul was born spiritually curved toward sin and earthly things. No human power could correct it. Only Your grace was able to restore my soul so it loved You and desired Your heavenly blessings. I had the power to deform myself by various sins. You alone were able to reform me. Just as an Ethiopian cannot change his skin or the leopard its spots (Jeremiah 13:23), so I was not able to do good because I was fully devoted to doing evil.

You, my God, converted me, and I am converted (Jeremiah 31:18). After I was converted by You, I repented. After I came to understand, I struck my breast (Jeremiah 31:19). I was dead in sin, and You made me alive. I was able to contribute as much to my conversion as a dead person is able to contribute to his resurrection (John 6:44; John 11:43). If You had not drawn me, I would never have come to You. If You had not awakened me, I would never have watched for You. If You had not enlightened me, I would never have seen You. Sins were sweeter to me than honey and honeycomb. That they are now pungent and bitter, I owe to You, the one who gave me my spiritual taste. Virtuous works were more bitter to me than gall and aloe. That they are now pleasing and delightful, I owe only to You, the one who changed my corrupt fleshly judgment by the Spirit. I went astray as a sheep that was lost (Isaiah 53:6); I turned to the way of iniquity. But You, Good Shepherd, sought me and led me back to the flock of the saints.

Only recently have I recognized You, the true light, because there were great, dark clouds before my vain eyes that prevented me from seeing the light of truth. Recently, I have recognized You, the true light, because I was blind and loved blindness and walked through the darkness of sin toward the darkness of hell. But You, my illuminator, sought the one who was not seeking You. You called the one who was not calling to You. You converted the one who was not converted to You. With a voice full of power, You said, "Let there be light in the inner parts of this heart," and there was light. I saw Your light and recognized my blindness. For that immeasurable kindness, I will praise Your name forever.

AMEN.

IX

THANKSGIVING FOR THE FORGIVENESS OF SINS

O ETERNAL AND MERCIFUL GOD, I owe You great thanks and give it to You. When I came, You did not cast me away (John 6:37). Instead, You immediately received me and with great mercy forgave me all my sins. Kindest Father, I was that prodigal child who squandered his inheritance through extravagant living (Luke 15:11). I polluted the gifts of nature. I rejected the gifts of grace. I deprived myself of the gifts of glory and eternal life. I was destitute and hungry. When I hungered, You fed me with the heavenly bread of grace. I was naked and destitute of anything good. You clothed me again with a robe of righteousness and made me rich. I was lost and condemned, but because of Your grace, You gave me eternal salvation. Having mercy on me, You attended to me. You embraced and kissed me (Luke 15:20) by sending Your beloved Son, who is by Your side (John 1:18), and the Holy Spirit, who is the kiss of Your mouth (Song of Songs 1:2).

The Son and the Spirit are the greatest witnesses to Your immeasurable love. You clothed me with the finest robe by restoring original innocence to me. You placed a ring on my hand by sealing me with the Holy Spirit.

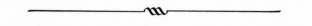

You shod me with shoes by equipping me with the Gospel of peace (Ephesians 6:15). For my sake, You killed the fatted calf by offering up to death for me Your beloved Son. You feasted and delighted me by restoring joy to my heart and true peace to my conscience (Psalm 51:14). I was dead, but through You, I returned to life. I wandered, but through You, I returned to the right path. I was destroyed by poverty, but through You, I returned to the wealth I had previously enjoyed.

Polluted by so many sins, covered by so many faults, corrupted by so many iniquities, in Your righteous judgment, You could have rejected me. But Your mercy abounded more than my sins. Your goodness was greater than all my iniquities. How often I closed the door of my heart to You when You knocked. Therefore, by Your righteous judgment, You could also have closed to me the door of Your grace at which I was knocking. How often I have closed my ears so I would not hear Your voice when You called. Therefore, by Your righteous judgment, You could also have closed Your ears so You would not hear my voice sighing for You.

But Your grace was more abundant than all my transgressions and faults. You received me with outstretched arms (Isaiah 65:2). You swept away all my iniquities as a cloud (Isaiah 44:22), and You cast all my sins behind Your back (Isaiah 38:17). You remember my sins no more and receive me with the full embrace of Your mercy. For this immeasurable kindness, I will give You thanks throughout eternity.

AMEN.

X

THANKSGIVING
FOR PRESERVATION
IN DOING GOOD

O LORD, to You be honor and glory and blessing and thanksgiving (Revelation 7:12). You not only mercifully receive me when I repent, but also grant me the ability to keep from sinning and to live a life more free from error. What good would it be to be free from sickness if a worse relapse followed? What good would it be to be absolved from sin unless the grace is given to live a pious life? You, most faithful God, perform the duties of a faithful and skillful doctor in healing the mortal wounds of my soul. You heal them by the wounds of Your Son. There is danger that the healed wounds will be reopened, but Your Spirit prevents this with grace like a poultice.

After receiving the forgiveness of sins, so many people return to their former way of living. By repeating their sins, they offend God all the more grievously. We see so many who were freed from the yoke of sin only to return to the bondage that once held them. So many of those who have been led out of the spiritual Egypt look back to its fleshpots of carnal pleasures

(Exodus 16:3). After recognizing Christ, they flee the defilement of the world but become entangled in it again as they return to their former evil ways (2 Peter 2:20). They were freed from the bonds of Satan through conversion. Trapped again by Satan's bonds, they hold fast to the deception of evil spirits. Their last state is surely worse than their first (Luke 11:26). It would have been better for them not to have known the way of righteousness than, having known it, for them to turn from the holy commandment delivered to them (2 Peter 2:21). They are like dogs that return to their vomit or like pigs that wallow in muck after they are washed (2 Peter 2:22).

The same can happen to me if You do not keep me on the good path through Your powerful grace and the effective working of Your Holy Spirit. The same evil spirit that captured them attacks me. The same world that seduced them entices me. The same flesh that secured them lures me. Only Your grace protects me against these attacks and furnishes me with the power necessary for victory. Your strength supplies the power I need in my weakness (2 Corinthians 12:9). You give my spirit the strength to restrain the passion of the flesh. Whatever is good in me comes from You, the font of all good things, because in me, by nature, there is nothing but sin. I have to acknowledge that all the good works I do—which are nevertheless impure because of the corruption and imperfection of my flesh—are gifts of Your grace. I will give You thanks forever because of Your immeasurable gift to me.

AMEN.

XI

THANKSGIVING FOR ALL THE GOODS OF SOUL, BODY, AND PROPERTY

O ETERNAL AND MERCIFUL GOD, I give You eternal thanks that You have not only given me body and soul, but also have provided me with many gifts of soul, body, and possessions. You, O highest Wisdom, teach knowledge to all people (Psalm 94:10). Therefore, if I experience anything that is good, this shows Your abounding grace toward me. Without Your light, my mind is darkness. Without Your grace, my will is captive. Any mental capability and knowledge I have comes from Your mercy. Knowledge enlightens the soul. Divine grace enlightens knowledge. Whatever we know is learned either from the light of nature or from the revelation of the Word. Both come from You. You are the light of eternal wisdom. Surely whatever we know comes to us from You as a gift.

O unfailing Font of life, You are my life and my length of days (Deuteronomy 30:20). O eternal Health, You are the strength of my body and the vigor of my power. We do not live by bread alone but by every word that proceeds from Your mouth (Deuteronomy 8:3; Matthew 4:4). Bread alone does not keep us healthy and strong. Medicine alone does not keep us from illness. No, we are kept by every word that proceeds from Your mouth. A calm and peaceful conscience keeps the body healthy. True piety brings a calm conscience. From You, O highest Good, comes true piety, an unshakably calm and peaceful conscience, and the physical health for which I long. Any physical thing I possess beyond these basics I owe to Your kindness. Indeed, I do not merit a single crumb of bread, much less all the great earthly things that You shower on me. When people possess these earthly things, we say, "They have had good fortune." But they are really gifts of Your grace. Nothing is more blessed than to use these gifts in service to others and to give them away. You have made me Your partner in this happy matter of giving gifts by granting to me a greater share of earthly possessions. You sowed in me the seed of Your grace so it may grow to become a harvest of kindness toward others. You have committed to me great wealth in earthly possessions so I have the means to do good to my fellow servants. Streams of material blessings flow to me from You, the Font of all good things. Whatever I am, whatever I have, whatever I give to others, I confess that all of it comes from Your kindness. For Your boundless mercy, I give You eternal thanks.

AMEN.

XII

THANKSGIVING FOR THE SACRAMENT OF HOLY BAPTISM

O ETERNAL AND MERCIFUL GOD, Father, Son, and Holy Spirit, I give You humble thanks. In the washing of Holy Baptism, You cleansed me from all sin, received me into the covenant of grace, and made me an heir of eternal life. I recognize it as Your gift that I was born of Christian parents and brought by them to the heavenly font. How many thousands of infants are born in the far reaches of paganism and die in their sins without this saving sacrament. The only thing that separates me from them is Your abounding grace. I am every bit as guilty as they are. Only participation in Your grace separates me from them.

How great is Your goodness that You found the one who was not even seeking You. You listened to the one who was not yet praying. You opened the door to the one who was not yet knocking (Matthew 7:7). Your mercy is far greater than any praise I could render. Your mercy is beyond my comprehension. I was baptized in Your holy name (Matthew 29:19). Your name was invoked on me. I was received into the heavenly family and made a child of the heavenly Father; Christ became my brother. I became a temple of the Holy Spirit. Baptism is a holy and heavenly washing; therefore, when I was baptized, I was washed clean and purified from all my impurities. Baptism is a washing of rebirth and renewal (Titus 3:5). Through Baptism, I have been reborn and renewed by the grace of the Holy Spirit. Everything Christ, my Savior, merited by His holy obedience and by the shedding of His precious blood He entrusts to the saving font of Baptism. Thus Baptism is like being sprinkled with the blood of Christ. The precious blood of Christ cleanses me from all sins (1 John 1:7) and makes me whiter than snow in God's sight (Psalm 51:7).

Through Baptism, O eternal God, You established an eternal covenant with me. The return to Baptism always stands open, a return made by true and earnest repentance. You have wedded me to Yourself for eternity in justice and righteousness, in grace and mercy (Hosea 2:19). In Baptism, You gave me the guarantee and seal of the Spirit (Ephesians 1:14). Therefore, You will not cast me away from Your face. Instead, You will remember Your promise and bring me to the heavenly wedding celebration. As the heavens were opened at Jesus' baptism, my mediator and head (Matthew 3:16), so You opened to me the door of paradise when I participated in that same Baptism. As the Holy Spirit descended on Christ at His baptism and as the voice of the heavenly Father stated that this is the beloved Son, so I have been made a partaker of the Holy Spirit and an adopted child of God by participation in that same

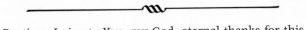

Baptism. I give to You, my God, eternal thanks for this
immeasurable kindness.

AMEN.

XIII

THANKSGIVING
FOR
THE SACRAMENT
OF THE ALTAR

MOST HIGH GOD, I owe You great thanks that in the sacred mystery of the Supper, You feed me with the body and blood of Your Son. What in heaven or on earth is more precious and excellent than this divine body, personally united with Your Son? Where is there a more certain testimony and pledge of Your grace than in the precious blood of Your Son, poured out for my sins on the altar of the cross? This, the price of my redemption, You give to me as the firmest testimony of Your grace toward me. As often as I have, through sin, fallen from the baptismal covenant, so often does a return to it stand open to me through true repentance and the salutary use of this Supper. It is a Sacrament of the New Testament. It blesses me again and again with new gifts of grace. Life itself dwells in this body, and this life restores me to eternal life and makes me alive. Through the shedding of this blood, satisfaction for sins was obtained. Thus drinking it ratifies the remission of my sins.

Christ speaks, and the truth speaks: "Whoever feeds on My flesh and drinks My blood has eternal life, and I will raise him up on the last day" (John 6:54). "I am the living bread that came down from heaven. If anyone eats of this bread, he will live forever" (John 6:51). The eating that Christ commends is that of faith. True faith is absolutely necessary when approaching the Supper for sacramental eating so that which was instituted for life is received by us for life. Therefore, I approach this heavenly Meal with true faith, firmly convinced that the body I eat is the one given into death for me, that the blood I drink is the blood shed for my sins.

From now on, I cannot doubt the forgiveness of sins because it is affirmed by my partaking of the price that was offered for my sins, the very blood of Christ (1 Peter 1:19; Revelation 1:5; 5:9). From now on, I cannot doubt the indwelling of Christ because it is sealed for me in the imparting of His body and blood. From now on, I cannot doubt the assistance of the Holy Spirit because my weakness is strengthened by such a support. I do not fear the plots of Satan because this angelic food strengthens me to do battle. I do not fear the lures of the flesh because this life-giving and spiritual food strengthens me by the power of the Spirit. I eat and drink this food so Christ may dwell in me and I in Christ. The Good Shepherd will not allow the sheep, fed by His body and blood, to be devoured by the infernal wolf. He will not allow the strength of the Spirit to be overcome by the weakness of my flesh. Praise, honor, and thanksgiving to You, O kindest Savior, forever.

AMEN.

XIV

THANKSGIVING
FOR PROTECTION
FROM EVIL

O ETERNAL AND MERCIFUL GOD, I give eternal thanks
to You that so far You have guarded me from countless
evils and provided me with the protection of Your holy
angels. Your gracious acts by which You have protected
me from evil are even more numerous than the acts by
which You give good things to me. Whenever I see others suffer evils of body and soul, I acknowledge Your
kind mercy toward me. If, indeed, I am free from such
cares and evils, I owe this only to Your goodness.

How great is the power of the devil. How great is
his deceitfulness. Every time that wicked spirit, our
powerfully cunning enemy, has tried to condemn me, I
have been able to flee his net and find safety behind the
shield of Your kindness and the protection of the angels.
Can anyone count the traps of the devil? Who can count
the times You have protected us from his traps? When I
sleep, Your providential eye watches over me to prevent
that hellish enemy, who walks around like a roaring
lion (1 Peter 5:8), from surprising me with his traps and
powers. When Satan attacks me with his temptations by

day, the strength of Your right hand comforts me in the kindest way and prevents that deceitful tempter from enticing me into his snares. When a countless army of evils threatens me, the camps of Your angels (Psalm 34:7) surround me like a wall of fire (Zechariah 2:5).

Even the most trifling and insignificant creature threatens me with various dangers. How great and boundless is Your kindness that You keep me safe from them. My soul and body are inclined to fall into sin. Because this is so, kindest Father, You rule my soul by Your Spirit, my body by an angelic shield. You command Your angels to guard me wherever I go and to support me with their hands so my feet are not dashed against a stone (Psalm 91:11–12). Because of Your mercy, I am not destroyed. New dangers surround me every day, therefore Your mercies are new to me every morning (Lamentations 3:22–23). You do not slumber or sleep, O faithful and watchful Keeper of soul and body (Psalm 121:4). Your grace is the shade at my right hand that keeps the scorching midday rays of open and harsh persecution from striking me down and guards me from the calamities and hidden ambushes of the night (Psalm 121:6). You watch over my coming in, direct my going forth, and govern my going out (Psalm 121:8). For this kindness, I will sing praise eternally to You and to Your name.

AMEN.

XV

THANKSGIVING
FOR
THE ETERNAL PROMISE
OF SALVATION

HEAVENLY FATHER, I thank You that You give me not only the free forgiveness of sins and the inner renewal of the Spirit, but also the sure promise of eternal life. Your goodness is so great that You give me, an unworthy sinner who has so often tried and tested Your mercy, the confidence of a heavenly hope and the certainty of the hope of an eternal, palatial dwelling in heaven. The benefits of this eternal life are so great that they cannot be measured. They are so plentiful that they cannot be numbered. They are so vast that they have no end. They are so precious that no value can be assigned to them. How great, therefore, is the undeserved goodness and kindness You have shown to me in blessing me with the sure promise of these benefits here in the debtor's prison of this life.

The apostle of truth testifies that by hope I am already saved (Romans 8:24). The same apostle fully guarantees that this hope does not disappoint (Romans 5:5). Then why do storms and tempests of doubt so often strike my heart, the boat in which Christ sails? You have given to me the promise of salvation, O God, and You are the faithful God (Psalm 31:5). How can I still doubt whether Your words of promise are immovably and unchangeably certain? That promise is free. In no way does it depend on the merit of my works. I can be as certain about the benefits promised to me by Your grace as I am about those things I see with my eyes. You feed me with the body and blood of Your Son. You seal me with the internal certainty of faith granted by the Holy Spirit. How could You confirm the promise of salvation to me by a more certain testimony or a more precious pledge? In the Supper, I know that You are with me in the tribulations of this present life (Psalm 91:15). Will I not also enjoy Your presence in the most blessed comfort of eternal life? If You give me so much while I live in the peasant's hut of this world, how much more will You give me in the palace of heavenly paradise?

Everything that You have promised to me for that future life and for which I now hope is as certain to me as all those things that You have provided for my use in this life. Your mercy and truth are great toward me, and they endure forever (Psalm 117:2). Your mercy precedes and follows me (Psalm 23:6). It precedes me in justification and follows in glorification. It precedes me and helps me to live a godly life. It follows so I may live with You forever. For all this, I will proclaim Your mercy and truth to this generation.

AMEN.

PART III

CONCERNING MEDITATION
ON OUR NEED

MEDITATING ON OUR NEED reveals that we possess nothing that is spiritually good. Therefore, it teaches us to reject all faith in our own power. It teaches us to flee to our only help, the divine mercy promised to us because of Christ. When we consider all our many needs, our hearts are raised to God. They ask Him to put to death the old man and to renew the new man. This work of God is needed daily by all those who have been reborn. This renovation consists of faith, hope, love, humility, patience, long-suffering, chastity, and the preservation and increase of all other good qualities. We are to seek these from God with earnest prayer. Every day we are assaulted by the flesh, the world, and Satan. Every day our flesh incites us to love earthly things. Every day the world assaults us with its hatred and Satan batters us with his plots. Therefore, we must pray daily to the Lord of hosts, our highest judge, to give us contempt for the world, denial of self, victory over the world, preservation in all difficult situations, true peace for the soul, victory in temptation, and preservation from the devil's plots. Finally, because in the hour of death and judgment we need God's help above all else, we must humbly pray every day for a blessed end to this life and for a blessed resurrection to eternal life.

I

PRAYER
FOR THE MORTIFICATION
OF THE OLD MAN

O HOLY AND MERCIFUL GOD, Father of our Lord Jesus Christ, I beg You in the Holy Spirit, for the sake of Your Son, to powerfully work in me and put to death the old man. I need this every day so I can be made strong in You according to the inner man. Sin dwells in my flesh (Romans 7:17). Give me the strength of the Spirit so I will not allow sin to rule me (Romans 6:12). You set my hidden sins in the light of Your countenance (Psalm 90:8). I ask You to bring them to light in my heart so I may recognize them, regret them, and humbly seek their forgiveness.

I am not yet completely free from the indwelling of sin. Please be gracious, I ask, and grant me freedom from the guilt and condemnation of sin. The law of sin in my members is warring against the law of my renewed mind (Romans 7:23). Give me the grace of Your Spirit so I may take captive the law of sin and not be captive to the old law of the flesh. The flesh lusts against the Spirit, and the Spirit against the flesh (Galatians 5:17). Indeed, the spirit is willing, but the

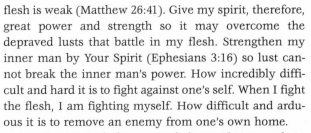

flesh is weak (Matthew 26:41). Give my spirit, therefore, great power and strength so it may overcome the depraved lusts that battle in my flesh. Strengthen my inner man by Your Spirit (Ephesians 3:16) so lust cannot break the inner man's power. How incredibly difficult and hard it is to fight against one's self. When I fight the flesh, I am fighting myself. How difficult and arduous it is to remove an enemy from one's own home.

Unless You clothe me with heavenly strength in this war, I am afraid that I will certainly be defeated by the hidden plots of the enemy. Strike down, burn, cut, and kill the old man so I can flee from this flattering fraud and seduction. Grant that daily I die to myself so the lures of the flesh will not draw me away from the true life that is in Christ. Inflame the fire of the Spirit in my heart so I may offer to You as a sacrifice the beloved child of my soul, which are depraved lusts and my own will. Flesh and blood cannot receive the inheritance of the kingdom of God (1 Corinthians 15:50). May they die in me so I will not be excluded from the kingdom of heaven. Those who live according to the flesh will die; those who by the Spirit kill the deeds of the flesh will live (Romans 8:13). Those who belong to Christ crucify the flesh with its desires (Galatians 5:24). Pierce and crucify my flesh, O Christ, You who were pierced and crucified on the altar of the cross for me.

AMEN.

II

PRAYER
FOR THE PRESERVATION
AND INCREASE OF FAITH

O LIVING AND ETERNAL GOD, You have kindled in my heart the light of true and saving faith. Because of Your kindness, I humbly beg that You mercifully preserve and increase my faith. I sometimes experience weakness in faith. I am tossed around by waves of doubt. I humbly cry out with the apostles for You to increase my faith (Luke 17:5). My heart places before You Your Word: "A bruised reed [You] will not break, and a faintly burning wick [You] will not quench" (Isaiah 42:3). I bear my treasure in an earthen vessel (2 Corinthians 4:7). I carry the little torch of faith hidden in a fragile container. I can do nothing but commend its keeping to You with earnest prayer on bended knees, daily and humbly praying for its increase. Make me a partaker of the heavenly light of faith in the darkness of this life and world. Your Word is light and life. Be gracious to me and help me cling with true faith to Your Word and become a true child of light and life through You. May the comfort of Your Word prevail in me against all the trials of Satan, against the contradictions of the world, even against the thoughts of my own mind. One word of Scripture is worth more than heaven and earth because it is more solid than heaven and earth (Luke 21:33). Work in me through Your Holy Spirit that I may more firmly believe Your Word and place understanding and reason in submission to faith (2 Corinthians 10:5).

Your promises are free and do not depend on my worthiness or merit. I can rest in them with the surest faith and trust in Your goodness with my whole heart. Through faith, Christ dwells and lives in my heart (Galatians 2:20; Ephesians 3:17). Preserve in me, therefore, the free gift of faith so my heart may be and always remain the dwellingplace of Christ. Faith is the seed of all good works and the basis of a holy life. Preserve and confirm me in this faith, kindest Father, so my spiritual harvest and dwelling will not suffer injury. Strengthen my faith so it overcomes the world and the prince of the world. Brighten the light of my faith so daily it spreads brighter beams ever further (Matthew 5:16). Preserve it amid the darkness of death so it may light before me the path to true life. Govern me by Your Holy Spirit so faith will not be lost by consenting to the lusts of the flesh and by indulging in sins against conscience. Confirm in me the good work that You began so, persevering in faith, I may obtain the inheritance of eternal life (Philippians 1:6).

AMEN.

III

PRAYER
FOR THE PRESERVATION
AND INCREASE OF HOPE

O OMNIPOTENT, ETERNAL, AND MERCIFUL GOD, I beg
You, because of the holy wounds of Your Son, preserve
in me the support of a living hope. Sometimes my heart
is tossed around like a ship on the sea. Grant me the
sure and firm anchor of hope (Romans 15:13; Hebrews
3:6; 6:19). I ask You, the God of hope and all consolation
(2 Corinthians 1:3), to hold me steady as I am tossed
around by temptations and doubts. The hope within me
can be as sure and immovable as the truth of Your
promises. I depend on Your promises. You will not leave
me without help. I trust in Your kindness. You will not
leave me without comfort. I know in whom I have
believed and am persuaded that He is able to keep what
I have committed to Him until that day (2 Timothy
1:12). I am absolutely persuaded that You who have
begun a good work in me will also complete it until the
day of Jesus Christ (Philippians 1:6).

Three things cause me to fall down before You in
praise. Three things calm my anxieties and give direc-
tion to my vacillating heart. These three things are the

love by which You adopted me as Your child, the truth of the promise, and the power to deliver what You have promised. This is the rope of three strands that You send down from the heavenly kingdom to me in this prison so You may lift me up and draw me within sight of Your glory. This hope is the anchor of my salvation (Hebrews 6:19). This is the narrow way leading to paradise (Matthew 7:13–14). Meditation on Your adoption makes me hope. Meditation on Your promise brings peace to my heart when I hope. Meditation on Your goodness prevents me from despairing of Your mercies. Meditation on my feebleness prevents me from hoping in my power and merit. The less my hope is fixed on the unstable and shifting sands of the temporal help of people or earthly things, the more firmly and surely it is established on the immovable and solid rock of Your promises and heavenly things. Unite my heart with You so I increasingly draw myself away from the world and cling to You with my whole heart.

I flee to You as to the throne of grace (Hebrews 4:16) and the altar of mercy, to the ark of the covenant and the refuge of freedom (Exodus 21:12), to the rock of strength (Psalm 18:2; 92:15; 1 Corinthians 10:4) and the gate of righteousness (Psalm 118:19–20). In me there is nothing but sin, death, and condemnation. In You there is nothing but righteousness, life, salvation, and comfort. I despair of myself, but I hope in You. Because of what I am, I am struck down. Because of what You are, I am raised up. Let the difficulties of this life greatly increase. Let Your life-giving comfort be present and lift up the one who hopes in You. Tribulations produce endurance, endurance character, and character hope.

Now hope does not disappoint (Romans 5:3–5). In You, O Lord, have I hoped; may I never be disappointed, even into eternity (Psalm 31:1, 17).

AMEN.

IV

PRAYER
FOR THE PRESERVATION
AND INCREASE OF LOVE

O ETERNAL AND MERCIFUL GOD, You are love itself
(1 John 4:16). Grant me the riches of true and sincere
spiritual love. My heart is cold and earthly. O Fire, O
Love, burn in me. My heart is hard and stony. O Rock,
O Love, soften me. My heart is full of the thorns of
anger and the briars of hatred. O kindest Father, O
Love, purify me. I love You, O God, my strength, my
rock, my fortress, my liberator, my God, my shield, and
the horn of my salvation (Psalm 18:2). Whatever I see
in creation that is good and excellent, I find all the
more abundantly and more excellently in You, who are
the highest good. So I will love You above all things,
with my whole heart. I acknowledge in You an abundance and excellence of good qualities. The more I go
to You, the better it is for me because nothing is better
than You. I am able to go to You not by walking with
physical feet, but by a loving desire of the heart. If I
desire beauty, You are the most beautiful of all. If I
desire wisdom, You are the wisest of all. If I desire riches, You are the richest of all. If I love power, You are the

most powerful of all. If I love strength, You are the strongest of all. If I love honor, You are the most glorious of all.

You loved me from eternity. In return, I will love You for eternity. You loved me by giving Yourself to me. In return, I will give back to You, through love, all that I am. Inflame my heart. Make every creature worthless to me. May You alone become the sweet desire of my soul. You desire to unite human nature to Your Son by an inseparable union. How much more fitting is it, then, that my heart be united to You by an inseparable bond of love. Divine love drew Your Son from heaven to earth, bound Him to a pillar to be whipped, and fastened Him to a cross to die. Should not such burning flames of love lift my heart from earth to heaven and bind me inseparably to You, the highest good? If I were to love earthly, worthless, and temporary things, I would treat both You and myself unjustly. You have made me worthy of so much honor and have given me such great promises by allowing me to love You.

When I love You, a sincere love for my neighbor is also born in my heart. Whoever loves You, O highest Good, also keeps Your commandments (John 14:15) because the presence of good works is the proof of love. Therefore, because You have commanded us to love our neighbor, no one sincerely loves You who does not pay the debt of love to one's neighbor (1 John 4:20). Indeed, whoever our neighbors may be, You were so concerned for them that You wonderfully created them, mercifully freed them, and most generously called them to fellowship in Your kingdom. In You and because of You, I am to love my neighbor, who is honored by You and given such glory. Strengthen and increase in me this true and sincere love, You who are eternal and changeless love.

AMEN.

V

PRAYER
FOR THE PRESERVATION
AND INCREASE OF HUMILITY

OMNIPOTENT AND MERCIFUL GOD, You bitterly hate all arrogance. Help me to be a rose of charity and a violet of humility so I may spread a fragrant aroma through works of love and think humbly of myself. What am I in Your sight, O Lord? Dust, ashes, a shadow, nothing. Therefore, because I am nothing in Your sight, grant that I consider myself nothing in my own eyes. Push back the inborn, swelling pride of my heart so I receive the dew of heavenly grace. The rivers of Your grace do not ascend up lofty mountains; instead, they flow down to the low-lying valleys of the humble heart.

I have nothing but weaknesses and transgressions. Whatever is good in me has come to me from the font of Your goodness. I can claim for myself nothing that is good because in and of myself I have nothing good. The more highly I think of You, the more unworthy I must consider myself. Far be it from me, O kindest Lord, to be arrogant concerning the gifts You have given me and to despise others because of them. You have placed a treasure chest of Your gifts in the shrine of my heart.

You have placed in that treasure chest gifts, traits, and abilities of Your choosing and number. Far be it from me to take credit for them or to claim to have deserved them. I am unworthy.

By Your Spirit, kindle the flame of piety and charity in my heart. Grant that I am able to cover my heart with the ashes of humility. How insignificant is the praise that one person gives to another. How insignificant is the praise one person uses to glorify another. The one who is great in Your sight, O great Creator, is truly great. The one who is pleasing to You is pleasing to the one who assigns a value to all things. But we do not please You unless we displease ourselves.

You are the life of my life. You are the soul of my soul. Therefore, I leave my life and soul in Your hands and cling to You completely with a humble heart. May Your eminence regard my lowliness. May Your highness regard my worthlessness (Psalm 113:4–7). Why do I desire to be praised by the world? Nothing in it is pure. Why do I glorify myself so much? The yoke of sin oppressively weighs me down. May a holy fear pierce my heart like a spike so it will not be puffed up with the most dangerous illness—spiritual pride. May my countless sins always be before my eyes, but may my good works, whatever sort they are, be forgotten. I am troubled by the memory of my sins more than I am pleased by the glory of any impure or imperfect good work that I have done. In You alone do I rejoice and glory. You are my joy and glory for eternity.

AMEN.

VI

PRAYER
FOR THE GIFT AND
INCREASE OF PATIENCE

O OMNIPOTENT, ETERNAL, AND MERCIFUL GOD, with humble sighs I implore You because of Your grace to grant me true and sincere patience. My flesh always desires what it wants, that is, what is easy and fleshly, but it refuses to suffer misfortune patiently. I ask You to restrain powerfully in me this inclination of the flesh and to prop up my weakness with the strength of patience. O Christ Jesus, teacher of patience and obedience, instruct me by the Holy Spirit so I may learn from You to deny my own will and to bear patiently the cross placed on me (Matthew 11:29).

You suffered more painfully for me than I suffer under anything that You place on me. I have merited harder punishment than the punishment that You inflict. You bore a thorny crown and the weight of the cross. You sweat blood and trod the winepress of wrath because of me (Isaiah 63:3). Why then should I refuse to take up patiently such a small measure of suffering and affliction? Why should I shirk from being conformed to Your suffering in this life (1 Corinthians 15:49; 2 Corinthians

3:18; Philippians 3:21; Hebrews 13:13; 1 John 3:2)? You drank from the torrent of suffering in life (Psalm 110:7). Why should I refuse a meager sip from the cup of the cross? I have merited eternal punishment because of my sins. Why should I not suffer fatherly reproof in this world (Deuteronomy 8:5; Hebrews 12:7)?

Those whom You knew from all eternity, before the foundations of the world were laid, You also predestined to be conformed to the image of Your Son in this life (Romans 8:29). So if I do not patiently bear this conformation to the cross, I despise Your holy and eternal plan for my salvation. Grant that this be far from me, Your most unworthy servant. It is to prove, not to punish, that You exercise me with various trials. When you place the cross and tribulation on me, You also grant me an equal amount of understanding and comfort. And the punishment never exceeds the reward. The sufferings of this life are not worthy of comparison to that heavenly consolation, which You grant already in this life, and to that heavenly glory, which You promise for the future (Romans 8:18). I know You are with me in tribulation (Psalm 91:15). I should rejoice over the presence of Your grace instead of being saddened over the burden of the cross placed on me.

Lead me on whatever path You desire, O best Master and Teacher. I will follow You through thorns and briars, but draw me along and sustain me. I bow my head so You may place on it a crown of thorns. In doing this, I am absolutely convicted that one day You will place on it an eternal crown of glory.

AMEN.

VII

PRAYER
FOR THE GIFT AND
INCREASE OF GENTLENESS

O KINDEST LORD, with great love for humanity, You invite us to repent and with long-suffering patience You await our conversion (Romans 2:4). Give me the riches of long-suffering patience and gentleness. When my neighbor does me the slightest harm, the fire of anger seethes in my heart. With humble sighs, I ask You by Your Spirit to put to death this habit of my flesh. What harsh reviling, harsher scourging, and harshest murdering Your beloved Son bore for my sake. When He was attacked by the reviler, He did not return the reviling (Luke 23:39). Instead, He committed everything to the one who justly judges all things (2 Peter 2:23). What arrogance it is, what obstinacy, that I, wretched and mortal, of the ashes and dust of the earth (Genesis 18:27), cannot bear the slightest harsh word or overcome the offense of my neighbor with a gentle heart.

"Learn, learn from Me, for I am gentle and lowly in heart," You cry out, O most excellent Christ. With humble sighs, I implore You to take me into that practical school of the Spirit so I may learn gentleness. How I offend You, kindest Father, with many serious sins. I need daily forgiveness for them. Therefore, because I am a human creature, why should I harbor anger against another person, then dare to demand pardon from You, Lord of heaven and earth (Sirach 28:3)? Would it not be foolish to be unmerciful to a person who is like myself, then to ask forgiveness of my sins from You, Lord? I cannot hope for the forgiveness of my own sins if I cannot forgive my neighbor's petty faults (Matthew 18:35).

O kindest Lord, great in mercy and long-suffering patience, give me the Spirit of patience and gentleness so I do not immediately become angry when my neighbor offends me. Instead, help me flee from that anger as from an enemy of the soul. If I carelessly become angry, help me to lay aside that anger quickly. May the brightness of the sun not set on my anger (Ephesians 4:26) so it will not depart as a witness to my rage. May sleep never fall on me when I am wrathful so sleep will not wrathfully hand me over to its sister, death.

If I want to retaliate against an enemy, why do I not turn against my own anger? Surely it is my greatest and most harmful enemy because it kills the soul and makes me liable to eternal death. Give me control of my mouth and wisdom in governing the actions of my life so I will not offend my neighbor by word or deed. Grant that I, through good deeds, may be a fragrant rose to my neighbor, not a piercing thorn of offenses and slanderings. O good Jesus, grant that I walk in the footsteps of Your gentleness and love my neighbor with a sincere heart.

AMEN.

VIII

PRAYER
FOR THE GIFT AND
INCREASE OF CHASTITY

O HOLY GOD, You love modesty and chastity and vigorously hate lewdness. I pray to You through Christ, the chaste bridegroom of my soul, to work in me true inward and outward chastity of soul and body, of spirit and flesh. Extinguish the fire of depraved lust in my heart. May a holy fear of You crucify my flesh so it will not be ruined in the wantonness of lust. May heavenly love carry my soul to You so it does not love to cling to earthly filth. Pour out on me the rivers of divine grace so those rivers will extinguish the flames of lust, just as water snuffs out flaming arrows. My soul was created in Your image and restored through Christ. I would inflict the greatest injury on myself if I would blacken the brilliant character of my soul with the soot and stain of shameful passion.

Christ dwells in my heart (Ephesians 3:17). The Holy Spirit dwells in my heart (1 Corinthians 3:16), fills me with the strength of His grace, and gives me gifts so I am holy in spirit and in body (1 Corinthians 7:34). Without holiness, no one will see You, purest Light

(Hebrews 12:14). May the loss of and injury to chastity be as detestable and hateful to me as the hope of seeing Your heavenly glory is desirable and lovely to me. The Holy Spirit is grieved by a spark of filthy talk (Ephesians 4:29–30). How much more is He grieved by the raging fire of lust? The appetite for lust is full of anguish and folly. The act is full of abomination and disgrace; it ends in sorrow and shame. Its flame rises to heaven, but its stench descends to hell. Why should I desire to throw open the door of my soul to this disgraceful enemy and receive it into the inner chambers of my heart?

O holy and mighty God, Lord of hosts, give me the strength of the Spirit to overcome the enemy that struggles in me and against me. Help me to avoid not only the illicit embrace of another person and disgraceful outward acts, but also free me from inner flames and desire for another. You require not only a pure body, but also a clean heart. With Your holy, penetrating eyes, You see the inner as much as the outer person. O Christ, who was crucified for me, crucify my flesh and its lusts.

AMEN.

IX

PRAYER FOR THE DISDAIN OF EARTHLY THINGS

O HOLY GOD, heavenly Father, I call on You through Your beloved Son and through the Holy Spirit to draw my heart away from earthly things and to lift its desires toward heavenly things. As fire naturally rushes upward, so the spiritual fire of love and devotion in my heart is inclined to rise toward heaven. Just what are these earthly things? They are more fragile than glass, more unpredictable than the sea, more fleeting than the wind. I would be a fool to place my trust in these things and to seek in them true peace of the soul. Even if unwilling, in death a person must desert all earthly things. Work in me so I willingly desire to forsake them before death. Put to death in me the love of the world so a holy love of You may spring forth. Guard me with the help of the Holy Spirit so I will not love this world, which will only corrupt my heart.

The form of this world is passing away (1 Corinthians 7:31). Its momentary glory is passing away; the destruction of heaven and earth is near. Change my heart so I may be a lover of the life that remains forever, not of this world that flees so quickly. Everything in this world amounts to the lust of the flesh, the lust of the eyes, and the pride of life (1 John 2:16). It is worthless to love the cravings of the flesh. It is dangerous to indulge in the lusts of the eyes. It is harmful to choose the pride of life. Those who are full of the earthly slop of pigs cannot truly love Christ, the heavenly bread of life (Luke 15:16). Those who are captive to the love of this world cannot freely raise their hearts to God. Where the vessel of the heart is full with the love of this age, there is no room left for God.

Extinguish in me, O God, the desire for earthly things. Take away the bonds that hold me captive to the love of worldly things. Purge and cleanse my heart so I may love You with a sincere love and cling to You with my whole heart. Why should I love those things that are in the world (1 John 2:15)? They cannot satisfy the desire of my soul. My soul was created for eternity; only eternal things can satisfy it. Worldly things cannot in the slightest way return the love I give them. My soul will love eternal things because it will dwell with these things for eternity. I will send ahead the desires of my heart to the place where an eternal glory has been prepared for me. Where my treasure is, there my heart will be also (Matthew 6:21). Give to me the wings of a dove (Psalm 55:6) so I may be lifted to You on high and be hidden in the clefts of the rock (Song of Songs 2:14). Do not allow the diabolic hunter to capture me in the trap of love for the world and draw my soul back to earthly things. May the whole world become bitter to me so Christ alone may become sweetness to my soul.

AMEN.

X

PRAYER
FOR THE DENIAL OF SELF

O Jesus Christ, Son of the living God, in Your Word You exclaim: "If anyone would come after Me, let him deny himself and take up his cross and follow Me" (Matthew 16:24). I beg You through Your most holy death and crucifixion to perfect in me the denial of self that You require. I know it is easier to forsake all creation than to deny self. I humbly beg You to accomplish in me that which of myself I do not know how to achieve. May the desires of my own will be stilled within me so I am able to hear Your divine admonition. May the weed of self-love be rooted out of my heart so the sweetest plants of divine love may grow within me. May I die totally to myself and my lusts so I may live totally for You and Your will. My will is changeable and erratic, fickle and unstable. Grant that I subject my will to Yours and that I cling unflinchingly to You, the only changeless and continuous good.

Divine power increases in us only when natural powers fail. Only when our own will has been put to death are our works done in God (John 3:21). Only when we are brought to nothing and disappear do we truly exist in and live in God (Acts 17:28). O true Life, put to death my will so I may begin truly to live in You. Anything in us that commends us to God and makes us pleasing to Him must descend from God Himself. Thus everything good must be ascribed to God alone, and that which is His must be left to Him. Whatever shines and gleams in us proceeds from God, who is the eternal and unchangeable light that lightens the inborn darkness of our minds. Thus may our light so shine before people, not that we are glorified but that God is glorified (Matthew 5:16). Kindle in my heart, O Christ, the true light, the light of true understanding. Work in my heart, O Christ, the true glory of the Father, the denial of my own honor and glory. It is better for me to be nothing in You and receive Your everything than to be something in and of myself and have nothing. Where I am not, there I am happier.

My weakness longs to be strengthened by Your might. My nothingness reaches for Your strength. May Your holy will be done on the earth of my flesh so Your heavenly kingdom may come in my soul (Matthew 6:10). Put to death in me the love and honor of self so the coming of Your kingdom may not be hindered. If our consummate good is that we love God, then absolute evil must be for us to love ourselves. If the free giving of one's self is a stipulation of true good, self-love is a great evil because it selfishly arrogates that which is its own and which belongs to others. If all glory is owed to God alone, then honoring one's self is the greatest theft. Such an act ascribes to itself things that really belong to another. Extinguish my habitual desire for self-love and honor, O Christ, the one who is blessed for eternity.

AMEN.

XI

PRAYER
FOR VICTORY
OVER THE WORLD

O OMNIPOTENT, ETERNAL, AND MERCIFUL GOD,
Father of our Lord Jesus Christ, grant me the grace of
the Holy Spirit so I may obtain the victory over all the
world's temptations. The world assaults me with hatred,
enticements, and perverted examples. Teach me to
regard the hatred shown to me by the world as insignificant, to avoid the world's charms, and to avoid imitat-
ing the world's depravities. What can the world's hatred
possibly do to me if Your grace protects me like a
shield? If You, my God, embrace me with love, what
harm can befall me, even if everyone attacks me with
hatred? On the other hand, if You pursue me with the
anger of Your wrath, what will it benefit me if everyone
loves me? The world is passing away, and the world's
hatred is passing away. Only the grace of God does not
change.

Remove confused fear from my heart, O God, so I
do not dread the world's hatred and persecutions. Plant
in me a fully confident soul and vigorous spirit so I
learn to think no more of earthly hatred than if it were

a fleeting cloud. Why should I fear those who kill the body but are not able to kill the soul? Instead, I will respect and fear Him who is able not only to destroy the body, but also the soul in the eternal fire of hell (Matthew 10:28). Our faith is the victory that overcomes the world (1 John 5:4). By faith we look forward to future joy so we can endure the adversities of the present age (Romans 5:1ff.). By faith we rest in divine goodness so we can bear the hatred of others. The world not only assaults me with its hatred, it also tries to lure me with its enticements. It has a stinging tail, but it also has a charming face. O Christ, give me the taste of sweet heavenly joy so all love of the world dies within me. My soul has a taste for things corrupt; it grasps for earthly things. Contempt for worldly enticements seems bitter to my soul. But You, who place the proper value on all things, have taught me to reject the world's charms. You have determined to lift my soul toward heavenly matters. Turn my heart away from the enticements of the world. Thus when I am turned to You, I might enjoy true spiritual delights.

Of what benefit is the empty glory, the short-lived joy, the trivial power to people who loved the world but are now dead? Of what benefit are the momentary pleasures of the flesh and the abundance of false wealth? Where are those who were with us a few days ago? Nothing remains of them but ashes and worms. They ate and drank without care. They finished their lives drunk with carnal joy. Now their flesh is fodder for worms, but their souls are tormented by eternal flames. All their glory has withered and dried up like the grass of the field (Psalm 103:15; 1 Peter 1:24). Prevent me,

O Lord, from entering their paths. I do not want to come to the same miserable end. Lead me to victory over the world and to the crown of heavenly glory.

AMEN.

XII

PRAYER FOR COMFORT
IN ADVERSITY AND
TRUE PEACE OF CONSCIENCE

O KINDEST FATHER, God of all hope and comfort (2 Corinthians 1:3), grant to me life-giving comfort and true peace of conscience in all the difficulties of life. My heart is full of anxieties, but Your comforts are able to delight my soul (Psalm 94:19). All the comfort of the world is empty and futile. In You alone is strength and support for my soul. All sorts of misfortunes weigh heavy on me, but Your encouragement and comfort lighten the burden. Nothing in all creation can bring me down and sadden me so much that You cannot gladden me by Your Spirit of joy (Psalm 51:12). No adversities can so surround and capture me that my heart cannot be freed by Your grace. The heat of various afflictions harasses me, but the taste of Your sweetness brings me cool consolation. The tears stream from my eyes, but Your gracious hand wipes them away (Revelation 7:17). Just as You allowed Stephen, the first martyr, to see Your gracious face even as he was being stoned (Acts 7:56), so also You allow me, wretch that I am, the full enjoyment of Your comfort though I am surrounded by misfortune. Just as You sent a consoling angel to Your Son in the most bitter agony of death (Luke 22:43), so also You send me Your sustaining Spirit in my struggle. Without Your strength, I would break under the weight of the cross. Without Your help, I would be destroyed by the attack of numerous adversities.

Extinguish in me the love of the world and created things so the misfortunes of the world and the change-ableness of created things will bring me no bitterness. Those who in their hearts cling to the world and created things will never be able to partake of true and undis-turbed peace. All earthly things are subject to the contin-ual variations of change. Those who do not cling with undue love to the things of this present life will not be tormented by overwhelming anxiety when these things are lost. Please, O God, cast out the love and desire of the world so that as You filled the widow's jar through the prophet Elijah, the soul forsaken of earthly comfort may be filled with the oil of joy (2 Kings 4:3; Psalm 45:7). All earthly things may be thrown into disorder, changed, and rolled back and forth, but You are the immovable rock and most solid stone of my soul. Can a beggarly and weak "thing" disturb the peace of the soul that I possess, that is sure and immovable in You (Psalm 73:25)? Can the waves of the world, even of its most turbulent seas, overthrow the rock of my heart (Psalm 18:2; 19:14), which I have firm in You, the highest and unchangeable good? Surely Your peace surpasses all understanding (Philippians 4:7). That same peace also will overcome every attack of mis-fortune. I beg You with humble sighs for that inner peace.

AMEN.

XIII

PRAYER FOR VICTORY
OVER TEMPTATIONS
AND FOR SAFE-KEEPING
FROM THE DEVIL'S PLOTS

GOD OF SABAOTH (Isaiah 6:3; Romans 9:29), powerful and merciful God, be with me so I do not succumb to satanic temptations and plots. Guarded by Your presence and supported by Your help, make me victorious over them. There are fears within me and conflicts outside of me (2 Corinthians 7:5). Inwardly, the devil wounds my soul with the poison and fiery darts of temptation (Ephesians 6:16). Outwardly, he harasses me with adversities and a thousand traps. He is like a serpent because of his treacherous deception, a lion because of his violent aggression, and a dragon because of his cruel oppression. If he dared to attempt to make himself commander of the heavenly army, will he keep himself from me, a common soldier? If he did not think twice to oppose the very Head (Matthew 4:3), is there any wonder that he attempts to destroy a weak member of the mystical body?

I have no power that can sustain me against this armed force. I have no wisdom by which to escape the deceptions and nets of its thousandfold traps. With humble sighs, I turn to You. Your power knows no bounds. Your wisdom is immeasurable. Be with me, O Christ, most powerful lion of the tribe of Judah, so in You and through You I am able to overcome this infernal lion (Revelation 5:5). You have fought and won for me, now fight and win in me so Your strength may be made perfect in my weakness (2 Corinthians 12:9). Illumine the eyes of my mind so I can see these satanic traps. Direct my feet so I can flee the devil's hidden snares. When I gain the victory in temptation, I have proof of my heavenly regeneration. The presence of Your grace confirms the promise of victory. Prepare and arm me with the power of Your might (Ephesians 6:10) so in this battle of the war, I am able to stand firm and hereafter judge that enemy by whom I am attacked (1 Corinthians 6:3).

As the dangerous plots of this enemy increase, I eagerly desire the help of Your mercy. The devil instills in me an insatiable desire for earthly things so he can lead me away from the way of righteousness and bind me by the shackles of covetousness. He inflames me with the spur of wrath so my heart burns within to bring injury to my neighbor. Out of nowhere, the devil incites me to love and lust for pleasures, then he inspires jealousy and ambition in my soul. Before he casts me headlong into sin, he persuades me that sin is lighter than a feather, lighter than a leaf on the air. As soon as he casts me headlong into sin, he repeatedly asserts that sin is greater than heaven and earth and heavier than the balance of divine mercy. Finally, I am driven to despair. If I cannot see such numerous and great plots of this enemy, how can I possibly guard against them by my own power? Therefore, I flee to You, my courage and my eternal rock of strength.

AMEN.

XIV

PRAYER FOR A BLESSED END TO THIS LIFE AND A BLESSED RESURRECTION TO ETERNAL LIFE

O JESUS CHRIST, Son of the living God, crucified and raised again for us, by Your death, You destroyed death. By Your resurrection, You merited for us a blessed resurrection to eternal life. You are one God with the Father and the Holy Spirit. I ask and beg You with my whole heart to grant me a blessed departure from this wretched life and a blessed entrance to eternal life on the day of resurrection and judgment. I know that an end to my life has been divinely appointed. I also know that judgment follows after death (Hebrews 9:27). Stand by me in death, You who died for me on the cross. Protect me in the day of judgment, You who were unjustly judged. When this earthly tent of mine has been destroyed (2 Corinthians 5), bring my soul into the dwelling of my heavenly home. When my eyes are darkened in the struggle of death, shine in my heart with the light of saving faith. When my ears are closed in the hour of death, cheer and console me with Your inner encouragement. When the cold sweat bursts forth from my dying members, remind me of Your bloody sweat that burst forth as the perfect payment for my sins and the remedy against the evil of my death (Luke 22:44). In this sweat, Your fervor for our redemption is manifest, in the blood, the price for our redemption, in its flowing down, the sufficiency of the price paid.

When in that last struggle speech begins to fail, grant that through the grace of the Holy Spirit I am able to sigh to You. When those last difficulties press on my heart, stand by me with the consolation and help of Your life-giving grace. Receive me, destitute of the help of all creatures, into Your care and protection. I beg You through Your most holy wounds endured as You suffered on the cross to grant that I am able to overcome the fiery arrows of Satan with which he attacks me in death. I beg You because of the severest torments that You experienced during crucifixion to help me endure and overcome all the insults of the power of hell. May my last word in the light of this world be the same one with which You brought to completion all things on the cross: Please receive my spirit, which You bought back at such a high price, and commit it into Your hands (Luke 23:46).

May a blessed resurrection also follow a blessed death. In that day of severe judgment, exempt me from a harsh word, You who have protected me with Your assistance. May my sins remain hidden by the umbrella of Your grace (Psalm 32:1) and be cast into the depths of the sea (Micah 7:19). May my soul be bound up in the bundle of the living God so with all the elect I may reach the eternal fellowship of joy.

AMEN.

PART IV

CONCERNING MEDITATION
ON OUR NEIGHBOR'S NEEDS

MEDITATION ON OUR NEIGHBOR'S NEED encompasses the common well-being of church and republic. This is the fruit of the true and sincere love that gathers us into one mystical body under one head, Christ, and commends to us serious care for the church as a whole and for all its members. If a member of the body does not strive, according to its share, to preserve the well-being of the whole body, or if it does not suffer when a fellow member suffers, it is no true member. It is the same with the mystical body of Christ (1 Corinthians 12:12ff.; Colossians 1:24).

Therefore, whoever is a true and living member of the Christian church ought to pray daily (Acts 3:1; Romans 12:12; Ephesians 6:18) for the preservation of the Word; for pastors and hearers (Ephesians 3:14–21; Colossians 4:2–4); and for the government (1 Timothy 2:2), those under authority, and the household. These are the three institutions divinely established for well-being in this life and for the extension of the heavenly kingdom (Romans 13:1–6; Ephesians 6:4; 1 Timothy 2:1–4). We ought to pray also for relatives and benefactors to whom we are bound by a special tie. We ought to pray also for enemies and persecutors (Matthew 5:44; Romans 12:14) because their conversion and salvation should be our earnest desire. We ought to pray also for those who are afflicted and who suffer hardship because their misfortunes should move our souls.

I

PRAYER FOR
THE PRESERVATION
OF THE WORD AND THE
INCREASE OF THE CHURCH

O OMNIPOTENT, ETERNAL, AND MERCIFUL GOD, Father of our Lord Jesus Christ, by the Holy Spirit, You gather the church from the human race and preserve in it the most holy deposit of heavenly teaching. I humbly praise You and submissively ask that You preserve undefiled the saving doctrine of Your Word among us and daily extend more widely the bounds of the church. Out of Your boundless mercy, set alight for us in this dark world the light of Your Word. Do not allow it to be extinguished or obscured by the fog of human tradition. Give to us Your Word as salutary food for the soul. We ask that You would prevent Satan's deceit and people's corruption from turning Your Word into a poison for us. Put to death in us the corrupt lusts of the flesh that thirst after earthly things. Instead, may we taste the delights of that hidden manna (Revelation 2:17), the spiritual things of Your Word. But no one will experience its sweetness if it is not tasted. No one tastes it whose mouth is still full of the world's delights.

Your Word is a word of Spirit and of life (John 6:63), a word of light and grace. Take away fleshly desires and the corrupt feelings of our hearts so Your Word may enlighten us within and lead us to the light of eternal life. From the light of the Word arises in our hearts the light of saving faith. In Your light, we see light (Psalm 36:9). In the light of the Word, we see the light of Your Son. Just as that heavenly manna once fell in the wilderness in a saving dew (Exodus 16:31), so also by the hearing of the Word our hearts are filled with the fervor of the Spirit. This fervor inflames our cold, luke-warm flesh while moderating the heat of depraved lusts. May this holy seed of the Word take root in our hearts and, excited by the dew of the Holy Spirit, bring forth salutary fruit to produce an abundant crop.

O Lord, guard the vine that is Your church (Psalm 80:14) in which that seed is sown. Guard the fruit until it is harvested in eternal life. Surround the vine with the hedge of an angelic guard so wild boars and foxes cannot root it up by violent persecutions or deceitful seductions (Song of Songs 2:15). Erect in this garden, Your church, the high watchtower of Your paternal providence so You may keep it safe from all devastation (Isaiah 5:2). If it seems good to You to squeeze this vine's clusters of grapes in the winepress of the cross for a time and to subject them to affliction, may they first become ripe by the fervor of Your grace so they may produce the sweetest fruit of faith and patience. Whatever is placed on the young root is changed in the clusters of grapes into the sweetest juice of the vine. Cause our souls to change the ridicule, persecution, praise, and whatever else befalls us in this world into the wine of faith, hope, and love and into the fruit of patience and humility. Out of this church militant, carry us forward at last to the church triumphant. May this portable tabernacle be changed at last into the most beautiful and everlasting temple of the heavenly Jerusalem.

AMEN.

II

PRAYER
FOR PASTORS AND HEARERS

O JESUS CHRIST, Son of the living God, our only mediator and redeemer, You have been exalted to the right hand of the Father. You send pastors and teachers of Your Word (Ephesians 4:11). Through their work, You gather the church among us to Yourself. I humbly beg You, true God with the Father and the Holy Spirit, that You guide Your ministers in the way of truth and turn the hearts of their hearers to the true obedience of faith. There is no occupation of human life, no class of people, that is so subject to the hatred and plots of Satan as the ecclesiastical ministry of the Word. Therefore, protect the members of this ministry with the shield of grace and furnish them with patience so Satan cannot trap them.

Grant Your ministers the necessary knowledge and pious diligence in all activities so they first learn from You before presuming to teach others (James 3:1). Govern and enlighten their hearts by Your Spirit so they preach nothing other than Your Word. Grant that they shepherd the flock committed to them (1 Peter 5:2), a flock purchased and redeemed by Your precious blood (Acts 20:28). Make their motivation true and sincere love, not covetousness or ambition. May they shepherd the flock in thought, word, and deed. May they shepherd by the prayer of their soul, by the exhortation of the Word, and by example as they follow in the footsteps of the one to whom the care of the Lord's flock was commended three times (John 21:15). Rouse Your ministers to keep watch over the souls entrusted to them because they will give account for them at the last judgment (Hebrews 13:17). Whatever they advise as they preach the Word, may they first be diligent in this matter in their own lives so they do not labor in vain to arouse others. Whatever good works Your ministers encourage in others, may they first be zealous in these works by the fervor of the Spirit. May they first proclaim by their works whatever actions they exhort by their words.

Send forth into Your harvest faithful workers so they may gather a great harvest of saints (Matthew 9:38). Open the hearts of the hearers so they may receive the seed of the Word with the holy obedience of faith (Act 16:14). Grant to these hearers Your grace so they may guard the holy deposit of the Word with a pure heart. With patience, may they bring forth abundant fruit (Luke 8:15). May they hear attentively, may they hear carefully, may they hear fruitfully—otherwise the Word that is preached to them, because it has not been mixed with faith, will judge them on the last day (John 12:48). Show forth the express promise of Your grace: Your Word will not return to You void (Isaiah 55:11). Grant that the labor of the one who plants and the one who waters may be blessed (1 Corinthians 3:7). Grant Your protection so the infernal raven may not dig up the holy seed of Your Word from the field of people's hearts, nor the thorn of worldly pleasures and riches constrain it, nor the hardness of stone prevent it from bearing fruit (Matthew 13:4ff.; Luke 8:12ff.). Water that seed with the heavenly dew of Your grace, poured out from above, so the most abundant harvest of good works may spring forth. Bind together the hearts of pastors and hearers in the closest bond of love so they contend together for one another in prayer and encourage one another through their care.

AMEN.

III

PRAYER
FOR THE GOVERNMENT
AND THOSE
UNDER AUTHORITY

O OMNIPOTENT, ETERNAL, AND MERCIFUL GOD, Lord of hosts, You remove kings and set up kings (Daniel 2:21). All powers in heaven and on earth are from You (Colossians 1:16). In heaven, the angels worship You, archangels praise You, thrones revere You. Governing authorities are subject to You and revere You, dominions serve You (Romans 13:1–4), the powers fear You. With these holy and most powerful spirits, I join my prayers, such as they are, and humbly ask You to fill our earthly government with the spirit of wisdom. Protect it with the strength of Your might. Support with Your grace all Christian rulers so the more they encounter danger because of their high position, the more they will experience the abundance of Your kindness. Kindle in their hearts the light of heavenly wisdom so they recognize that they are subject to You, Lord of all, that they are Your vassals, and that one day they must give account for their governing.

May they strive for peace because they serve You, the Prince of Peace. May they strive for justice because they serve You, the most just Judge. May they strive to be merciful because they serve You, the kindest Father. May they be guardians of the Ten Commandments and of the church, which is downtrodden in this world. May they show goodwill and correct judgment toward those under their authority. Draw their hearts away from the splendor of earthly and miserable power so a forgetfulness of the heavenly kingdom and true piety does not creep up on them. Rule them by Your Holy Spirit so they do not become puffed up with pride and misuse the power granted to them. Grant that they carry out their official duties in such a way that they may rule without end in eternity with all the elect and pass from the most fleeting glory of this age to the eternal glory of the heavenly kingdom. Prevent them from exercising tyranny over Your people so, after wearing glittering clothing and elegant gems, they do not descend, naked and wretched, to be tormented in hell.

You willed us to be subject to Your representatives. Grant to us obedient hearts. Make us ready to serve with complete willingness so under the authority of Your representatives we may lead quiet and peaceful lives in all godliness and virtue (1 Timothy 2:1). May we show honor and obedience to those whom we acknowledge as possessing authority and power over us. May we comply with their honorable commands so by keeping these laws we may be partakers of true liberty. True liberty is, in short, to serve God, government, and law. O kindest God, may we honor with heart, word, and deed those whom You have willed to be Your representatives on earth. May the eyes of the government leaders be watchful and observant (Proverbs 20:8). May the ears of those under their authority be open and attentive. May the gates of heaven finally be open and unobstructed to both.

AMEN.

IV

PRAYER
FOR THE HOUSEHOLD

OMNIPOTENT AND MERCIFUL GOD, Father of our Lord Jesus Christ, in Your most wise judgment, You instituted the household in addition to the ministry of the church and the rule of government. I praise You and beg You with my whole heart to guard this holy nursery of church and republic. Grant to married and unmarried, widows and widowers, true holiness of soul and chastity of body. May the unmarried depend completely on You (1 Corinthians 7:34). May those who have been widowed continue in prayer day and night (1 Timothy 5:5). May husband and wife highly esteem each other with sincere love (Ephesians 5:25). May all serve You in righteousness and holiness with their whole heart. May the marriage bed be undefiled (Hebrews 13:4) and every soul unstained. May all who believe be violets of humility and lilies of chastity. May they be roses of charity and balsams of sanctity.

Bind together with the bond of chaste love the hearts of the pious who are married so they embrace each other willingly and continue in Your holy service. Guard them from the plots of Asmodeus (Tobit 3:8) so they do not burn with hatred for each other. May the wife be a helper for her husband and supply comfort in adversity (Genesis 2:18). May the strong bond of marriage be a holy mystery of the love between Christ and the church (Ephesians 5:32). The closer the fellowship of husband and wife, the more fervent may their zeal in prayer be. The more they are subject to peril and misfortune, with souls more closely joined, the more may they be engaged in piety and prayer.

Please stand by pious parents with Your grace so they bring up their children with holy admonition and discipline (Ephesians 6:4). May they acknowledge that their children, the fruit of marriage, are Your gift. May they offer them back to You through a pious and faithful marriage. May they place before their children an example of a holy life so they will not entangle themselves in the most grievous sin of causing others to stumble.

Bend also the hearts of the children so they show to their parents the obedience owed to them. May they be the fragrance of a heavenly paradise's little plants, not useless wood that is subject to the flames of hell. May they scatter about the most pleasant smell of piety, obedience, reverence, and every virtue so they do not fall into the detestable stench of sin and hell. May they remember the commandment to honor their parents. May they be roused to cherish their parents in return. May they remember to return to their parents the care they received so they will not fall into the abyss of misfortune (Ephesians 6:2–3). May parents and children worship You, true God, with united devotion in this life so they may praise You in eternal life with united praises.

May servants willingly obey their masters, serving them with fear and simplicity of heart, not only with eye-service or to please people. May they decide to render this service to Christ (Ephesians 6:5–6). In turn, may masters embrace servants with kindness so lawful authority does not lead to tyrannical cruelness. The household is a household church, highly esteemed by God and angels.

AMEN.

V

PRAYER FOR RELATIVES AND BENEFACTORS

O HOLY AND MERCIFUL GOD, from You descend abundant and various gifts. You have provided great assistance for this life through relatives and benefactors. I beg You to repay them with eternal rewards. I commend especially to Your keeping those whom You willed to be connected to me by a bond of nature and blood. With eager prayer, I entrust to You the well-being of those to whom I owe special love and care. Grant that my relatives may serve You with united and diligent souls so they may one day receive the unfading crown of eternal glory.

I can never give back a worthy gift to my parents, whom You gave to me. They are, next to You, the authors of my life. They trained me in true piety. Therefore, I humbly beg You, the source of all good and the rewarder of all kindness, that You repay their kindness with temporal and eternal rewards. May the example of Christ, Your Son, who in the agony of death commended to His disciple the care of His mother (John 19:26–27), teach me to be concerned for my parents until their last breath. May nature, in the example of the stork, teach me that continual service is owed to my parents. I commend also to You, kindest Father, the safety of my brothers and sisters and of all my relatives. May they be brothers and sisters of Christ. May they be heirs of the kingdom of heaven. May those whom You have joined with me in natural life be joined with me in the kingdom of grace. May those whom the ferocity of death has already separated from me be returned to me with eternal joy at the time of Your final coming. Make us all citizens of the heavenly Jerusalem, even as You have in this life made us members of the true church.

I heartily pray the same for all my benefactors, those to whom I owe care and the desire for their salvation. Receive into the eternal dwellings of the city above those through whom You have shown me such manifold and abundant kindness (Luke 16:9). My heart places before You the promise of Your Word that You, out of grace, desire to repay the drink of cold water (Matthew 10:42). How much more will those who generously present kindness to those in need experience Your generosity and kindness (Proverbs 19:17; Matthew 25:40)? Do not stop the flow of Your favor to those from whom so much kindness flowed to others. May the font of Your goodness continually flood over those from whom flooded such abundant streams of generosity. O most merciful God, cause those who have so abundantly sown carnal things to receive spiritual things with a great return on their investment (1 Corinthians 9:11). Fill with joy the souls of those who fill the stomachs of the hungry with food. May the fruit of their kindness not pass from them, though it come from passing goods. Give to those who give to others, Giver of all good, the one who is praised throughout eternity.

AMEN.

VI

PRAYER FOR ENEMIES
AND PERSECUTORS

O LORD JESUS CHRIST, only begotten Son of God, in Your Word, You have prescribed for us this rule of love: "Love your enemies and pray for those who persecute you" (Matthew 5:44). I pray also to You, the most generous forgiver of sins, for my enemies and for those who persecute the church (Luke 6:35). Give me the grace of Your Holy Spirit so I not only forgive my enemies from my heart, but also heartily pray for their salvation. Do not sharpen over them the stern sword of revenge; instead, anoint their heads with the oil of mercy. Extinguish in their hearts the hot ashes of wrath and hatred so they do not flame up into the infernal fires of hell. May they recognize that life is a quickly dissipating vapor and smoke (James 4:14), our bodies fleeting ashes and dust (Sirach 10:9). Then in their mortal bodies they will not bear immortal wrath nor receive the enemy of their soul into the feeble home of their earthen body.

May they recognize that this deep-seated hatred is their greatest enemy because it kills the soul and excludes them from participation in heavenly life. Enlighten their minds so they gaze into the mirror of divine mercy and recognize the ugliness of anger and hatred. Direct their wills so they are moved by the example of divine forgiveness and resist the inclination to be angry and to injure. Graciously allow that, as much as it depends on me, I may live peacefully with all people (Romans 12:18). Turn the hearts of my enemies to reconciliation. May we walk harmoniously on the path of this life because we hope for one place in the heavenly kingdom. May we not be separated on earth because we desire to live as one in heaven. We call on You, the one Lord and God of heaven. It is by no means right that servants of the one Lord are not united. We are one mystical body under Christ the head (Ephesians 1:22–23; 5:24). For members of one body to fight one another is disgraceful and dishonorable. For those whose faith is one and whose Baptism is one, it is fitting that they be one in spirit and soul.

I pray not only for my private enemies, but also for the public enemies and persecutors of the church. Turn them to the way of truth, O highest Truth. Avert their bloodthirsty efforts, O supreme Power. May the brightness of heavenly truth strike their eyes shut so the rabid furor for persecution is stilled in their souls. May they recognize that it will be in vain and dangerous to continue to kick against the goad (Acts 26:14). Why do they imitate the rage of wolves? They know that the blood of Christ, the spotless lamb, was shed for us. Why are they eager to pour out innocent blood? They know the blood of the Son of God was poured out on the altar of the cross. Convert them, O God, so they obtain the fruits of their conversion in this life and in the life to come.

AMEN.

VII

PRAYER
FOR THE AFFLICTED
AND THOSE
WHO ARE SUFFERING

OMNIPOTENT, ETERNAL, AND MERCIFUL GOD, You are the Savior of all, especially those who believe (1 Timothy 4:10). You have commanded through the apostle that prayers be offered for everyone (1 Timothy 2:1). On behalf of all who are suffering under affliction and hardship, I beg You to uphold them with the consolation of Your grace and to support them with the help of Your might. Clothe with heavenly power and strength those who sweat in the most grievous agony of satanic temptation. Make them partakers of Your victory, O Christ, powerful victor over the devil. May the refreshment of Your heavenly grace encourage those whose bones are dried up by the fire of sorrow. Uphold all those who fall and raise up all who are bowed down (Psalm 145:14). Be gracious in allowing illness so physical sickness may be a spiritual medicine. May those who are ill recognize that sickness is an attendant of sin and a forerunner of death. Give to them strength of faith and patience, O true

Physician of souls and bodies. Restore them to their former health, provided that it is advantageous to their eternal salvation.

Protect those who are with child; support those who are giving birth. It is You who bring infants from the confines of their mother's wombs and enlarge the human race by Your blessing. Be with those who are in the pains of labor, O Lover and Giver of life, so they are not oppressed with excessive pain. Nourish orphans who are forsaken of all help. Protect those who have lost their spouse because You who have called Yourself the Father of the fatherless and the Defender of the widowed (Psalm 68:5). May the tears of those who have been widowed break though the clouds and not be quieted until they reach Your throne (Sirach 35:15ff.).

Hear those who are in danger at sea and cry out to You. Give freedom to the captives so they may proclaim Your kindness with grateful hearts. Make firm those who suffer persecution for the sake of righteousness so they may be victorious over all their enemies and receive the eternal crown of martyrdom (Matthew 5:10). Help those who are suffering dangers and misfortunes so they may possess their souls by true patience (Luke 21:19) and, denying their own will, take up their cross (Matthew 16:24). As they take up their cross, may they follow Him in whom they believe and who died on the cross. Kindest Father, I specifically entrust to Your care those who are poised at the gates of death, those who hover between time and eternity and who wrestle with all their might with this last foe. Make them firm, O powerful Victor over death. Free them, O glorious Ruler of life, so they are

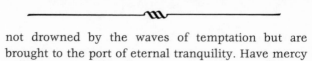

not drowned by the waves of temptation but are brought to the port of eternal tranquility. Have mercy on all, You who are the Creator of all. Have mercy on all, You who are the Redeemer of all. To You be praise and glory for all eternity.

AMEN.

ENDNOTES

1. Martin Luther, *Word and Sacrament I*, vol. 35 of *Luther's Works*, ed. Jaroslav Pelikan and Helmut Lehmann (Philadelphia: Fortress, 1960), 54.

2. According to August Tholuck, *Exercitium Pietatis Quotidianum*, which included *Meditationes Sacrae*, was produced to correct the deficiencies of Johann Arndt's *True Christianity*, but it never caught on with the public.The earliest edition available is *Meditationes Sacrae, ad veram pietatem excitandam Item Exercitium Pietatis Quotidianum quadripartitum. opera et studio Johannis Gerhardi, S.S. Theol. D. & in Acad. Ienens. profes. Francofurti ad Maenum Sumptib. Christ. Hermsdorfii 1655.* See "Gerhard, Johann," *Realencyklopädie für protestantishe Theologie und Kirche*, ed. Albert Hauck (Leipzig: J. C. Hinrichs, 1899), 6:554ff.

   For this translation, I used the second part of *Johannis Gerhardi Meditationes Sacrae Eiusdemque Exercitium Pietatis Ad Veterum Librorum Fidem Recensuit Hermannus Scholz, Gymnas. Guetersloh. Magist. Gueterslohae, Sumptibus C. Bertelsmanni. MDCCCLXIII [1863].* I also made frequent reference to the anonymous German translation of Johann Gerhard, *Tägliche Uebung der Gottseligkeit: Aus dem Lateinischen übersetzt* (St. Louis: M. C. Barthel, 1874).

3. Gerhard's original dedication included the "definition" of prayer that comprises the introductory chapter of this present translation. Following are some additional thoughts included by Gerhard in his dedication to Lord Heigel:

"With the publication of *Sacred Meditations* and the five books on *The School of Godliness*, I have tried to turn our hearts toward true piety and to advance the growth of the inner man. I also have completed a special manual with consoling meditations for opposing all kinds of temptations (see Gerhard, *Enchiridion consolatorium* [1611]), but I still needed to write a little book of prayers that would serve common people to the best of my ability. I was eager to complete this work, so it was easy for me to accomplish it. But I, too, am harassed by the problems and misfortune that beset every believer in this life.

"I nobly and honorably desire to dedicate and offer this book to you, a highly esteemed man of noble birth in the later years of your life, to express my thanks for the extraordinary kindness that you have shown to me in many ways. I also dedicate this book to you as a public testimony to your piety, a testimony offered before the learned, especially to the teachers and students of the churches and schools. With this testimony, I desire to show you worthy courtesy and proclaim your many virtues. I would run through your noble and distinguished praises more freely, but it is necessary to expound only on your virtues. When these virtues are known, praise proceeds voluntarily. Even if I spoke only of your virtues, I would be addressing them endlessly."

4. The theologian Johann Arndt (1555–1621) assembled such a list of terms to describe prayer in book 2, chapter 36, of *True Christianity*. In his list of appellations for prayer, Gerhard does not quote Arndt consistently, word for word, or in order. However, he obviously has Arndt's list firmly in mind. See Johann Arndt, *True Christianity: A Treatise on Sincere Repentance, True Faith, the Holy Walk of the True Christian, etc*, trans. by A. W. Boehm (1712; rev. by C. F. Schaeffer; Philadelphia: Lutheran Book Store, 1868), 290.

5. Christ has two natures, divine and human, in one person. Human nature was corrupted by original sin after the fall into sin and will be free of it again after the resurrection. Christ assumed a human nature. Although it was not a

sinful human nature, it was exactly like our human nature, including everything that defines it as such. Original sin, however, is not an essential part of human nature; it is an "accidental" corruption of this nature. "Satan cannot create a substance; he can only, with God's permission, corrupt accidentally the substance which God has created" (*Formula of Concord*, Epitome, I, 25).

Copyright © 1992, 2003 M. C. Harrison

Published by Concordia Publishing House
3558 S. Jefferson Avenue, St. Louis, MO 63118-3968

Manufactured in the United States of America

Original edition of Matthew C. Harrison's translation published as *Sacred Meditations* by Repristination Press in 1993.

Cover Art: Jesus Washing Peter's Feet by FM Brown
Tate Gallery, London/ET Archive, London/SuperStock

Woodcut images are used with permission from the
Pitts Theology Library, Emory University, Atlanta, GA

Jacket, cover and book design by Melissa Jarnagin, CPH.

Library of Congress Cataloging-in-Publication Data

Gerhard, Johann, 1582-1637.
    [Exercitium pietatis. English]
   Meditations on divine mercy : a classic treasury
of devotional prayers / Johann Gerhard ; translated
by M. C. Harrison.
      p. cm.
   ISBN 0-7586-0387-8
1. Meditations. 2. Devotional exercises. I. Title.
   BV4813.G4613 2003
   242' .8—dc21   2003005587

      2   3   4   5   07   06   05   04